The
Natural History
of a Garden

The
Natural History
of a Garden

Colin Spedding
Geoffrey Spedding

TIMBER PRESS
Portland · Cambridge

To the children of St Nicholas Hurst Primary School and the
former Head Teacher, Mrs Marion Morgan.

All photographs and drawings are by Colin Spedding except those on
pages 220, 221, 230 and 231 that were drawn by the children of St
Nicholas Hurst Primary School.

Published in 2003 by

Timber Press Inc
The Haseltine Building
133 S.W. Second Avenue, Suite 450
Portland, Oregon 97204, U.S.A.

Timber Press
2 Station Road
Swavesey
Cambridge CB4 5QJ, UK

Designed by Dick Malt

Printed in Hong Kong

ISBN 0-88192-578-0

Catalogue records for this book are available from the British Library
and the Library of Congress.

Contents

Colour plates follow page 128

Preface

Since I am fortunate enough to have a large garden, containing wild, wooded and boggy areas, with ponds, I have many opportunities for observing garden wildlife. Jackdaws nest in one of my chimneys, wasps in my roof space, bees (and even hornets) in the walls of my old cottage, and all three species of woodpeckers in my trees – all of which are impossible to miss. However, in September 1993, Carly Blake, a pupil at St Nicholas Hurst Primary School, which abuts one end of my wooded area, wrote to ask if the children could visit what they called 'the plantation'. I readily agreed and visits have since taken place every year, the early ones being led by teacher Kate Caton. It was only when these children started to visit my garden regularly that I began to look more systematically at the natural history all around me in order to make their visits more interesting. So, in a sense, they have opened my eyes to this world, as I hope I have helped to open theirs.

As a consequence, I have developed ways of allowing them – and others – to look through windows on the normally unseen world of nature in the garden. The most successful has been the placement of dustbin lids on long grass, under which nest voles, shrews, woodmice, bumble-bees and ants and where occasionally can be found grass snakes, newts and toads, as well as all the creatures normally found under stones and logs.

So I started writing this book in 1996 and it has grown steadily since then. I soon realized that although gardens vary enormously the principles and general approach I am advocating remain much the same. To illustrate this I persuaded my son, Dr G R Spedding, who has lived in Los Angeles for 20 years, to collaborate with me on the book as a whole and, in particular, to add the section on American Gardens in Chapter 1. The family dimension was increased when my daughter, Mrs Lucy Weston, who works with children of all ages, contributed her experience to Chapter 11. Subsequently, the children at St Nicholas Hurst School also discussed the chapter and offered their comments (and pictures). To avoid unnecessary wordiness in the text, the personal pronoun refers to me, except in the section on 'The American Garden' in Chapter 1.

Acknowledgements

It is a pleasure to thank especially my secretary, Mrs Mary Jones, for all her help in the preparation of this book from the beginning in 1996 to publication, and Anna Mumford, commissioning editor at Timber Press, for her help and encouragement during the publication process.

1 Gardens and Natural History

Although most people understand perfectly what is meant by the word 'garden', it is nevertheless almost impossible to define. It conjures up a plot of land growing plants, generally cultivated, with a peaceful atmosphere, intended to be attractive to people. Its purpose is pleasure, which is perhaps why Epicurus (whose views are usually associated with the pursuit of pleasure) taught in a garden. Yet we all know that a garden can be tiny or huge, orderly or fairly wild, formal or cottage, and with or without trees, water, hedges, ornaments, paths, seats and buildings. Most contain flowers, at least for part of the year, and many include grass; all contain animals, most of them small and generally unnoticed.

The appearance of gardens is probably what concerns most people, whether they are gardeners or not, yet appearance is only one of the pleasures to be derived from a garden: scent is often sought, and sound – as in leaves rustling in the wind, for example – is appreciated (though more rarely sought). All these attributes change with the seasons and vary with the site: soil type, rainfall, average temperatures, slope and aspect may all result in marked differences. Consequently gardens look different from each other according to location and each garden alters in appearance throughout the year.

Indeed, this seasonal variation is why gardens remain perpetually fascinating to a gardener: one reason for going out into the garden is to see what has changed. Watching plants grow and develop provides satisfaction at the results of past work and pleasurable anticipation of what is to come.

Some gardeners will take a close interest in particular plants, ones that they are introducing or cherishing; others will watch the changing shape and patterns of colours and foliage. Clearly, there are different ways of looking at a garden, and the purpose of this book is to suggest another vision – not that of the traditional gardener but that of a naturalist.

CHAPTER 1

Once you start thinking about ways of viewing a garden, you realize that the perception of a butterfly, a rabbit or a child would be quite different. This is sometimes due to properties of the eyes or the mind but there is also a general principle involved: you cannot really look at, or even see, all that is around you.

Look round your sitting-room; how many of the objects present can you possibly look at, or even be aware of, simultaneously? You have to be selective or your eyes and mind would become overloaded. For example, as we travel about we are all surrounded by numerous cars of all shapes and sizes, most of which we neither notice nor remember. But suppose that we have just decided to buy a particular make, say a Ford: from then on we notice every one we see and soon come to know the whole range of sizes, models and colours. In other words, we select information from what was always there, simply because we are looking for it, and gradually we become better at seeing it. It is the same in a garden – we see mainly what we are looking for and expecting to see. Thus a tour of a garden tends to resemble a visit to old friends.

However, this is probably not the way a child views it. A child is more likely to see it as a voyage of discovery, looking for trees to climb, banks to slide down, flowers to pick or grass to play on. The same is true of the naturalist, in the sense that a visit to a garden becomes a voyage of discovery, and the naturalist is looking for all living things. He, too, will mainly see what he is familiar with in places where he knows it may be found, but discovery is about seeing new things and finding out what they are and what they are doing.

The gardener tends to be mainly interested in the plants which, for the most part, will still be where they were last seen. The naturalist has a wider canvas which includes all the animals in the garden, and these are rather unlikely to have remained where they were last seen – although it turns out that there are interesting exceptions to this. So, a naturalist's way of looking at a garden can be an extension of the gardener's, adding other dimensions and thus interest and content.

This book explores this possibility but it has to offer more than this, since the gardener cannot suddenly, unaided, see things as a naturalist would. You have to know what might be there. And where, exactly? And when? And how can it be seen, recognized or watched?

And, since animals are shy and retiring, and can hear you coming, or see you first, are there signs of their presence that can tell you what was there before your arrival?

These questions are addressed in the following chapters. Although the intention has been to avoid a rather tedious cataloguing of species, some descriptions are essential: these have been framed to aid identification in the context of a garden, rather than providing the information a scientist would need to distinguish exactly which species is involved. This is not necessary for the enjoyment of the natural history of a garden and would, in any case, be quite impossible for the hundreds (or even thousands) of species that might be encountered.

Gardeners are already familiar with many of the main pests and it may not be necessary to know, for example, which of the 46 possible species of aphid in a typical British garden you are looking at. That is not to say that they can all be lumped together, either, but their strange relationships with the ants that 'milk' them may be more interesting to discover. It is even more interesting to find that there are probably only some five species of ants commonly found in British gardens, some of which 'milk' aphids that they keep entirely underground, feeding on plant roots. Even within a limited range of species, one of the fascinations of natural history is the range of numbers found: some are quite small but many are enormous (see Table 1.1).

For most people, the natural history of the garden opens doors and windows on a new world, one that has been there all the time and simply not seen. Revelation of this kind happens to children all the time and conjures up a sense of wonder that soon gets lost in familiarity. So a new, or different, way of looking at a garden can add a great deal but detracts not at all from gardening and the ways in which a gardener looks at things. Indeed, the greater the fondness for and interest in plants, the greater should be the interest in the animals that interact with them – sometimes as pests but often to their benefit. If you find this difficult to believe, imagine growing plants in a soil with no living organisms, or growing fruit with no bees, or coping with pests without all their unseen predators or parasites.

Of course, this new knowledge may change the way you garden. If you like to see goldfinches, you may think it worth leaving seedheads

Table 1.1 Some interesting numbers

(Such numbers only indicate the order of magnitude: variation is enormous)

m = metres; m. = millions

Eggs laid by 1 frog	1,000–4,000
Bees in a hive	50,000–80,000
Bumble-bees in a nest	200–400
Voles	Home range: male up to 1500 m² (1794 sq yd) female, up to 38 m² (45 sq yd)
Owls	Home range: >3 km² (2 sq miles)
Ants in a nest	A few hundreds to tens of thousands (depending on the species — up to 100,000 in the wood ant)
Wasp's nest	12,000 cells, 10,000 wasps (up to 25,000 in a season)
Snail teeth	15,000 per snail
Leather-jacket	Up to 247 per m² (295 per sq yd)
Grey field slug	Up to 1.235m. per ha or 124 per m² (500,000 per acre or 148 per sq yd)
Spiders in a field	Up to 6.3m. per ha or 630 per m² (2.5m. per acre or 753 per sq yd)
Insects currently living	10^{19} (10,000,000,000,000,000,000)
Humans (2002)	6.3 billions (thus there are 1.6 billion insects for each living person)

Seed production	Number of seeds per plant
Dock (*Rumex crispus*)	4,000 – 25,000
Toadflax (*Linaria vulgaris*)	29,000
Mullein (*Verbascum thapsus*)	700,000
Foxglove (*Digitalis purpurea*)	750,000

Number of legs

All insects	3 pairs
Centipede	15 – 51 pairs (exceptionally over 100 pairs in some species)
Millipede (c. 12 species in gardens)	up to 80 pairs
Pill bug	17–19 pairs
Woodlice	7 pairs

on plants to attract them, and even growing a few thistles; if you like butterflies, you may plant the species that supply them with nectar; if you want to control pests, you may welcome spiders; if you want a green woodpecker to visit your lawn, you may choose to leave the ants alone.

These animal examples may give the impression that natural history is only about animals. This is not so: originally, it meant all that is in nature, including animals, plants, rocks and other minerals. The focus is generally on living things, however, and the interest in the non-living parts of the environment is usually related to their role in support of plants and animals as homes, hiding places, nutrition, and so on.

The reason for emphasizing the animals here is that these are the living elements in the garden that tend to be less noticed by the gardener. Natural history, however, is mainly a field or outdoor pursuit. It is concerned more with the way organisms live in their surroundings than with taxonomy, although many early naturalists were great collectors of birds' eggs, butterflies and moths – now, fortunately, out of fashion, or even illegal. The reason for this relates to the stage of development of a subject. Initially, it is necessary to identify and catalogue what is there and to describe it all in unambiguous terms.

You can easily imagine how limited our experiences would be if you could only tell me that you saw a bird with a speckled chest eating a snail, breaking the shell by hitting it on a rock. If, on the other hand, you were to say that it was a mistle thrush, I would be surprised and say that I thought that only song thrushes did this. So, when naturalists first looked at nature, they had to concentrate first on naming things before they moved on to studying what they did, what they ate, what they were eaten by, how long they lived, how they reproduced and a whole host of such things. (The Chinese actually have a proverb: 'The beginning of wisdom is calling things by their right name.') The study of an individual thus widens out to include how it relates to its environment, including other species, and becomes 'ecology'.

All this applies to plants just as much as to animals but gardeners already know about the plants. Or do they? Most people tend only to think about the above-ground part of the plant. Gardeners, because they plant things, have a better idea of root systems – but they cannot see them growing and dying and being eaten by small creatures. Yet roots die off all the time, just as leaves do, and both depend on myriad mainly small organisms to recycle their organic matter and incorporate it into the soil. Fertility is not just increased by the application of fertilizer or manure, it is continually created by micro-organisms, earthworms and even root-feeding pests, such as wireworms and leatherjackets (where do they come from?). Even above ground, internal processes are not visible and many changes that are visible may not be noticed.

This is particularly true of trees. They tend to be ignored in the winter, yet the buds we associate with the spring are often present and fully formed in late autumn. In early winter, you can cut a pussy-willow bud in half and see all the silky, silver hairs tightly packed and ready for warmer weather. Also unnoticed go the thousands of caterpillars that may denude the oak tree of its first crop of leaves in the spring. Probably they would be considered undesirable, but these are what blue tits feed their young on.

Many people can identify trees only when they are in leaf, yet their shape, bark and buds are quite characteristic, as are the seeds – and, of course, all are often inhabited by tiny creatures. Some trees house larger occupants and, even in the winter, hole-nesting birds can be seen exploring potential nesting sites and trying them out for size. It is much more difficult to tell when birds that do not nest in holes are selecting nesting sites, but they may also do it well in advance.

Plants all have their own ways of ensuring that their seeds are spread and many of these involve animals. Gardeners tend not to allow plants to seed themselves, except for trees and shrubs, unless the seeds are decorative (as with many rose hips), but some of the mechanisms for propelling seeds into the air are extraordinary (for example those possessed by most of the cranesbill family – see Chapter 3). Everyone is familiar with wind-blown seeds, such as the dandelion. It seems a purely passive operation, but did you know that dandelion seeds will only blow away when the air is dry, and thus may act as useful weather forecasters? Seeds, of course, occur as something of a culmination of the growth and reproduction cycle.

All flowers have to be pollinated: who does that? Honey-bees would be the obvious answer, but bumble-bees work at lower temperatures and at the ends of the day, while moths are more useful for night-flowering plants. A host of beetles, flies and solitary bees are involved in pollination as well, quite apart from the wind. Shouldn't a gardener know who is doing all this work?

Growth is quite hard to define but growth in length (extension growth) is in many ways the most spectacular. Shoots can elongate at an astonishing rate: how does this happen? Often it is because all the cells are there waiting and only need to take up water in order to expand. But if this happened too soon, the vegetation might freeze. So why don't buds freeze – or the leaves of holly, ivy and green hellebore?

Trying to understand how it all works has to start with wondering and then investigating, but this is no fun if there is no way of discovering the facts. Part of the aim of this book is to trigger the wonder, stimulate the questions and provide some of the answers. However, in a world as complex as a garden, with so many different occupants, it is not possible to answer more than a fraction of the questions. A huge literature is available for those who wish to probe further, in any of the many directions indicated. Even this, though, is only a starting point; after all, there are whole books on, for example, dragonflies alone, with more being published. Consequently, it is not difficult to obtain identification keys – but it is virtually impossible to list them all.

The sheer number of species makes many people think that they will never be able to cope with memorizing such volume and variety, so they never start to study them. This is a pity – it does, after all, apply to most subjects (what about stars or novels or languages or gardening?). It is like all such apparently mammoth undertakings, such as climbing a mountain: the important thing is to take the first step. It is not necessary to know every species – it is often quite enough to be able to identify a group. Initially, it is enough to be able to distinguish dragonflies from damselflies, ryegrass from meadow-foxtail, butterflies from moths, spiders from harvestmen, or frogs from toads (and their spawn, which is quite distinct).

This is the approach that has to be adopted here, although quite often the number of species commonly found in the UK turns out to be very small, for example snakes (three), toads (two), moles (one), woodpeckers (three), bumble-bees (nine). That is, of course, for those found in the whole of the UK, but in addition, the number within your own garden will be even more limited. If you have bats flying round your house, there is no need to despair of identification because there are 32 species in Europe and nearly a quarter of all mammalian species are bats (that is, 951 species): it is most unlikely that you have more than, say, two. There is therefore, no attempt here to list all the species (or even all the genera) that may be encountered, and individual species are only identified and described to illustrate some specially interesting features.

Identifying groups of species is often quite easy. For example, did you know that:
(a) All insects have six legs?
(b) All spiders have eight legs (but so do mites)?
(c) All butterflies have knobs on the ends of their antennae?
(d) All moths have tapering, often feathery, antennae (with no knobs)?
(e) Caterpillars that move by 'looping' all belong to one family (the *Geometridae*)?

It is true that there are also confusing aspects. For example, many species have juvenile forms that are quite unlike their parents. Butterflies are insects and therefore have six legs, but everyone is aware that their caterpillars are quite different: they also have six 'true' legs but often have a number of 'false' legs (usually at the rear end) in addition. The first leaves of many plants look nothing like the ones that finally arrive and are characteristic of the species. Figure 1.1 shows some examples – but anyone who has grown peas or beans knows this perfectly well.

Figure 1.1 First and second leaves of some trees

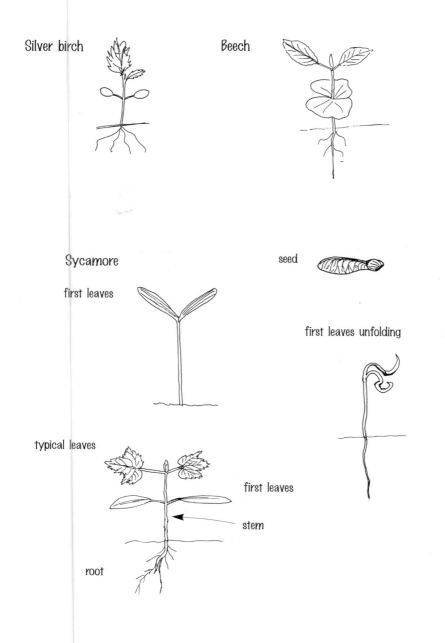

Silver birch

Beech

Sycamore

first leaves

seed

first leaves unfolding

typical leaves

first leaves

stem

root

Of course, it is much more complicated than that. A great many larval forms of butterflies and moths don't look like caterpillars at all, and even some adults look quite atypical (some moths are unable to fly, for example). A number of growths on plants look quite unlike the rest of the plant. These are often galls caused by minute wasps or flies: the gall is a growth of tissue stimulated by the presence of an insect egg and designed to isolate the invading organism, which is thereby provided with a source of food. Galls come in a huge variety of shapes and sizes (see page 50 and Box 7.5), some very attractive and some grotesque. If you cut one open, you will often find the grub inside that is responsible for it.

Birds often have juvenile forms. Young blue tits, once feathered, look like little adults but young British robins have speckled rather than red breasts until they are full-sized, when both sexes have red breasts. Green woodpeckers are spectacularly coloured, their reds, greens and yellows being quite bright, but the immature birds have a characteristic barred colouration not present in the adults. Wood-pigeons differ from other pigeons and doves not only by their broad 'padded' shoulders, but also by the white ring round their necks (see Box 1.1). But confusingly, their young do not acquire this feature for several months, before which they may resemble the adults quite closely in most other respects, including size. The time when the white neck patches are developed depends on the moulting period and this may be in mid or late autumn, depending on the date of hatching.

Wood-pigeons are quite big, noisy birds; their flapping departure from a tree is unmistakable. However, you rarely see a young wood-pigeon and the adults are extraordinarily wary, especially at nesting time. It is quite hard to catch a wood-pigeon actually building a nest, whereas rooks seem to draw attention to the activity; crows' nests, by contrast, although their nests are quite large and often noticeable, are usually built when you are not looking. If you watch closely, you gradually come to recognize behavioural patterns that are preparatory to nesting. Then, if you continue to follow the birds' movements, you may actually catch them at it. Of course, if they can see you, nothing will happen – they may even deliberately mislead you, flying into the wrong bush, for example – but, even if you are unseen, it requires great patience. You get the impression that if you look away for a

Box 1.1 Doves and pigeons

There is really no difference between doves and pigeons, but the term dove tends to be used for the smaller species. Many people are confused by this group although there are few species and they are, in fact, quite distinctive.

Wood-pigeon *(Columba palumbus)*

The largest pigeon, about 40 cm (16 in) in length, is often called the ring-dove because of the prominent neck patches (in the adult) that almost join to form a ring round the neck. The colour is predominantly blue-grey, with a black band under the tail and white bands across the tail and each wing. The legs are coral red.

Stock-dove *(Columba oenas)*

A smaller species about 33 cm (13 in) in length, the stock-dove has no white markings and its colour is darker with a mauve-pink breast and iridescent green neck.

The rock-dove *(Columba livia)*

This species is similar to the stock-dove but with two black wing bars and a whitish rump.

Turtle-dove (*Streptophelia turtur*)

A summer visitor, the turtle-dove is nearer 27 cm (10^{1}/$_{2}$ in) long, with red-brown upper parts marked with black, a dove-grey head and red eyes. The tail has long black feathers, the central one having a white tip.

The collared-dove (*Streptophelia decasoto*)

This species, which has spread rapidly, has a distinguishing black half-collar and pale dusty-brown upper parts. The tail shows a lot of white.

Nests

All nest in trees or shrubs and build relatively slight platforms of twigs except for the stock-dove, which nests in tree-holes. Male pigeons sit on the eggs by day and females take the night-shift.

Feeding

They all have crops in which they can carry and store food and they can all regurgitate this to the young. They can all secrete pigeon's 'milk' to feed the newly-hatched young. The proportions of the diet vary between species and seasons but all consume seeds (including cereals and many weed seeds), clover and other leaves, with the addition of animal food (especially small snails, woodlice and some earthworms) during the breeding season. The wood-pigeon is the only major consumer of tree buds and also takes ivy berries during the winter.

---

second, the bird has gone and you've missed the action.

Sometimes, the coloration of birds differs markedly between the sexes (for example mandarin and mallard ducks and drakes, bullfinches, blackbirds, chaffinches, pheasants) but not so in others (for example thrushes, wrens, British robins, tits, house martins, most owls and swans – although the male has a larger black 'knob' above the bill). How these latter ones tell each other apart, I have no idea. Perhaps we all look alike to them! Incidentally, it is often possible to tell what a bird feeds on by looking at the shape of its beak or bill (see Box 1.2).

Frogs and toads do not show marked differences between the sexes for most of the year but in the spring differences appear, both physically and, markedly, in behaviour. The males croak and grasp the females from behind, remaining in this 'piggyback' position until the eggs are laid. The skin of the females becomes covered with rough granules.

Very often, species can be distinguished by their eggs. This is well known for birds but is also true for most butterflies, lacewing flies, many snails and slugs, frogs, toads and newts, for example. It is also the case for most plant seeds and, where they are encased in nuts or embedded in fruits, these also have quite characteristic appearances. The sexual organs of plants are fairly easy to differentiate and both sexes commonly occur on the same plant. Not always, however (for example in some trees), and reproduction may then depend upon having both male and females trees in close proximity.

Looking at the natural history of a garden depends on – and develops – sharp observational skills, but, once acquired, they are habit-forming. This applies to more than the garden. It is remarkable that so many people are unaware of the small creatures living in or on

Box 1.2 Bird beaks and their diet

Beaks are used to find food and divide it up (birds have no teeth), to attack prey, for defence and for excavating holes (for example in trees, as with all the British woodpeckers). Nevertheless, in many cases, the nature, shape and size of the beak is associated with the nature of the food.

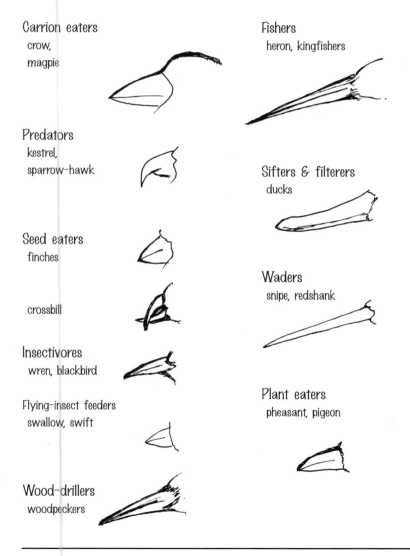

Carrion eaters
  crow,
  magpie

Predators
  kestrel,
  sparrow-hawk

Seed eaters
  finches

  crossbill

Insectivores
  wren, blackbird

Flying-insect feeders
  swallow, swift

Wood-drillers
  woodpeckers

Fishers
  heron, kingfishers

Sifters & filterers
  ducks

Waders
  snipe, redshank

Plant eaters
  pheasant, pigeon

the walls of their houses (for example zebra spiders – see below). Not only are they not seen but little thought is given as to what they are up to. For example, when butterflies are seen on puddles or on freshly deposited dung, the automatic assumption is that they are eating or drinking. But butterflies cannot eat; their only mouth parts are modified to form a coiled tube for drinking nectar. So are they after water? Not really, they are after the minerals dissolved in it, since nectar is rather deficient in this regard.

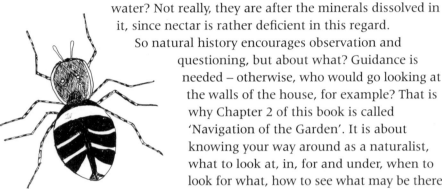

So natural history encourages observation and questioning, but about what? Guidance is needed – otherwise, who would go looking at the walls of the house, for example? That is why Chapter 2 of this book is called 'Navigation of the Garden'. It is about knowing your way around as a naturalist, what to look at, in, for and under, when to look for what, how to see what may be there, and what the most interesting garden features are likely to be. Chapters 3 and 4 then deal with the plants and animals to be found in gardens, but not just as lists and descriptions but how they live and die, grow, reproduce and, sometimes, care for their young. (This is not just a feature of birds and mammals but earwigs and spiders, too.)

Figure 1.2 Zebra spider (length 7mm/¹/4 in)

Chapter 5 explores what goes on in the soil and you could argue that some understanding of this is essential for a gardener. But, then, this is also true of the plants and animals. The plants are either wanted or weeds and the animals are mostly pests or beneficial.

Since gardens are so different at different times of the year, Chapter 6 deals with seasonal change, though this is a very crude way to describe the effect of passing time. Day and night are quite different and hot, dry days are different from cold, wet ones. In some cases, animal and plant activities and developments are confined to quite short periods. Some flowers open for only a few hours at a time: wolf spiders look after their young under their silken tents for only a few weeks in the year.

All these plants and animals interact with each other, each providing homes, food or enemies for the others. The networks so formed are the subject of Ecology (Chapter 7) and the outcome of all these interactions needs to be determined in a garden. After all, gardeners are seeking a particular outcome, wanting some species to thrive and others not. So control is important (see Chapter 8). Sometimes this is provided by the gardener, as water, sprays or fertilizer, but this is only operating at a superficial level on the surface of the garden. For the most part, species are controlling each other all the time, and intervention is better based on some understanding of how this balance of nature is arrived at.

Water is essential to life and is provided by rainfall, snow, dew, irrigation/watering or the water table, but it can also be a major feature like a pond or a lake. Chapter 9 describes the natural history of such bodies of water. It is quite astonishing how rapidly a pond is colonized by small creatures, for many pond-dwellers can fly very well, which is how many of them deal with pond-homes that dry out in summer. Others are so small that they are blown about by the wind and, in any case, can survive, in one form or another, in the dried-out mud that forms the bottom of the empty pond.

Quite apart from the inhabitants, ponds attract visitors, mainly to drink (birds, mammals, wasps and bees) and sometimes to feed or hunt (grass-snakes, frogs, herons and ducks). So water is one reason for animal visitors to the garden but, as Chapter 10 explains, there are many other reasons, including flowers, seeds, insects in soil and grass, aphids on roses and foliage for food.

Sometimes, in the case of animals with large ranges, such as foxes, deer, pheasants and most flying birds, a garden is just part of the range and when (or, more usually, if) you see them, they are just passing through. Often, you may see signs of them even when you do not see the animal.

In the case of birds, since most are active during daylight and flight takes place above ground, they are more noticeable and there is a very good chance of seeing them – if you happen to be looking during the very short time that they are visible. In addition, birds are often quite colourful and even a glimpse may reveal their identity. For example, a flash of white rump in a finch-size bird is usually a bullfinch; a clattering flight from a tree is a wood-pigeon; a dipping flight of a large greenish-yellow bird is a green woodpecker (though its 'laugh' is a more common means of identification); the mouse-like creeping of a tree-creeper up a tree trunk is unlike anything else, except the nuthatch which is more usually heading down, and is bigger and bluish-grey on the back instead of brown.

So it is for many other creatures. Recognition is often based on a very few give-away characteristics. With practise, one sees whole patterns of biological activity built up from partial glimpses.

Finally, Chapter 11 looks at gardens in a quite different way, through the eyes of children, and considers what a garden specially created for them would look like. This is partly based on the regular visits I receive from the neighbouring St Nicholas Primary School, to whom this book is dedicated. Small children, apart from their use of gardens as playgrounds and adventure parks, are naturally inquisitive and respond readily to the kind of 'voyage of discovery' approach I am recommending.

Up to this point, it is British gardens that have been under discussion but virtually everything in this chapter would relate to gardens anywhere in the world, in principle. What would be quite different, however, would be the particular species that occur. Most of the major groups of plants and animals would be represented, but by different species. Gardens almost everywhere would have insects, spiders and birds, for example, and, in many cases, they would be fulfilling similar roles. However, there are often differences in such features as the number of poisonous plants and animals: it is very important to know this if you are going to explore the inhabitants of a garden with which you are not familiar. Climate and seasons may be radically different, affecting species, numbers of individuals and their behaviour. To explore these differences and similarities, the next section of this chapter considers the natural history of an American garden.

The American garden

While this book was born in contemplation of an English garden, many of the general ideas can be extended to the similar examination of gardens everywhere. Here, we note some specific issues raised in thinking about gardens in the United States. One of the authors (GRS) has lived in Los Angeles for 20 years now, and has a garden there. Yet he was raised in English gardens (by CRWS no less!) and so some comments can be made on parts that need translation.

American is used here as simple shorthand for the United States of America. Inclusion of Central and South America together with Canada would carry us far afield indeed. The spectacular increase in range and diversity of native animal and plant species could not begin to be covered. Even as it is, the reader will recognize the practical difficulty in providing more than cursory coverage of the fauna and flora in the United States. However, this book is neither an encyclopedia nor a catalogue, and instead, it is the principles of organization and behaviour that most concern us.

First, the very notion of the American Garden seems much less concrete than its British counterpart. With such a diversity of climate, geography and wildlife, how can there be any such single thing? In the north-east of the country, average daily temperatures may not exceed 20°C (68°F) for more than a handful of days of the year. In the south-west, in California, there may be few daily averages below 10°C (50°F) all year. In central parts, there may be winter temperatures around –20°C (–4°F), while summer temperatures are regularly above 30°C (86°F), with 90 degrees humidity.

The range and annual variation of the fauna and flora vary widely as a result. And yet, does not the same hold for the differences between Scotland in the north-east and Cornwall in the south-west in the UK? Perhaps, but surely the range is not so great – and it seems as though there ought to be a bigger difference, more specific, more tangible; perhaps it is the rainfall. Few areas of the UK are without rain for extended periods. The comparative droughts that have appeared in the last 10 – 15 years may seem to refute this idea, yet their very measure is an indication of their rarity and in contrast to the usual dependability of an adequate rainwater supply over most of the country for most of the year. In Southern California, the annual rainy season lasts about six weeks, and outside this it basically does not rain. In the California coastal low-lying lands it does not snow, or sleet, and it almost does not rain. In Louisiana in the south and in Oregon in the north-west the rainy seasons seem as if they will never stop. Total rainfall in the year 2001 exceeded 200 cm (79 in) in Louisiana, while parts of southern California, Nevada and Arizona received less than 15 cm (6 in). So the tremendous variation in rainfall gives to the American climate and the countryside and garden it helps to create a variety that is not matched anywhere in the UK.

25

The second natural difference is in average population density. A large percentage of the countryside in the UK is modified for agriculture. In the United States, there are still uncultivated areas right next to large cities. In many parts of Los Angeles, the second largest city in the country, the family cat must be kept inside at night or be at risk from local coyotes that come down from the hills. There is a certain wildness that is much closer and that in the UK has been smoothed out over many years of significant human impact.

These differences can be seen to affect the species of plants and animals, most notably the larger ones, when the environment poses different challenges and offers different refuges or solutions (or lack thereof).

Origins

Historically, including up to the present, the local species have been affected by what is already there. North America was connected to northern Europe and South America to Africa 180 million years ago, in the Jurassic age. The age of the reptiles (including the famous giant ones) was in full swing, and the five classes of vertebrates (fish, amphibians, reptiles, birds and mammals) were already established. It was during this time that the Atlantic began to divide North America and Europe. In the Cretaceous age (135 million years ago) the earliest mammal orders, marsupials and insectivores, were appearing, and by the Eocene (54 million years ago) all the main mammalian orders were in place, their explosive (in geological time, note!) growth coinciding with the dramatic extinction of the reptiles.

Meanwhile, at about 150 million years ago, the number of similar species between the two regions was already decreasing significantly, and the main diversification of mammals occurred after the separation of the two land masses. Table 1.2 of notable haves and have-nots for the United States has several mammalian entries for this reason. The effective connection with Northern Europe was not actually broken until the Miocene (23 million years ago). All modern families of mammals, including the more recently differentiated giraffes, pronghorns, bovids (bisons, goats, sheep), hippos, elephants and hyenas were developed by the end of the Pliocene, about 5 million years ago.

Table 1.2 Some of the larger potential garden visitors notable by their presence or absence in North America

Present:

Gopher, beaver, jumping mouse, opossum, armadillo, tree porcupine, peccary, pronghorn, hummingbird, wild turkey, snapping turtle, musk turtle, terrapin, rattlesnake, gecko, iguana, gila monster, bear, coyote, alligator, tarantula, scorpions, mountain lion.

Absent:

Hedgehog, dormouse

Common principles, functions and adaptations

On the other hand, small-scale processes are quite universal, and will be little changed – processes of growth, photosynthesis, reproduction and death being largely similar. Even at a larger scale, similar ecological niches, if not populated by identical species will be occupied by equivalents that do similar things; they may behave similarly and may even look the same, either in basic form or in specialized features. For example, you can still guess at what a bird feeds on (thus accounting for some portion of its life-style) from the shape of its beak. The figures in Box 1.2 were drawn for British birds but need no editing for North America. Then, both countries have some species not found in the othe, for example the hummingbirds of the United States (see Box 1.3) and many more examples (see Table 1.2).

As humans, we are good at spotting differences, but from any neutral standpoint, the functional similarities between animals and plants in British and American gardens probably predominate. Adult insects all (without exception) have six legs, regardless of which side of the Atlantic they come from. All spiders have eight legs. Most beetles have hard wing cases, and dragonflies and damselflies rest their wings in the same (equally different) way. Ladybirds (or ladybugs) feed on aphids, woodpeckers drill holes in trees, blue jays bury nuts in the ground.

Box 1.3 Hummingbirds

The 17 species of hummingbirds that breed in the continental United States represent only five per cent of the total worldwide, and the number of species increases quite sharply towards the equatorial regions of South America. In the United States they are found mostly in the south-west, but the ruby-throated migrant, for example, is found all over the country to the east of the Rocky Mountains.

Hummingbirds have no counterpart elsewhere in the world, as no other bird can perform their characteristic trick of continuous hovering (although most birds must be able to do this for brief periods on take-off and landing). Aerodynamically, they can be considered as honorary insects, with whom they overlap in body mass (they are occasionally confused with sphinx moths). The comparatively small and pointed wings are unusually manoeuverable and can generate useful aerodynamic forces of high magnitude on both downstroke and upstroke. Their spectacular aerobatics are energy-costly, made possible by their natural fuel source.

Hummingbirds eat insects and energy-rich nectar provided by the characteristic red- or pink-flowering plants with which they have co-evolved. The flowers are often deep-throated, and the long beak must be inserted so deeply that the head or chest are marked by pollen from the specially designed overhanging or fringing stamens.

To locate a hummingbird, find some bright red flowers and then wait quietly, watch and listen. The high-pitched clicking sounds frequently betray the hummingbird's presence long before they are located by eye. If bees have nests to return to, then where do hummingbirds go? Females are associated with nests (begun with spider silk!) only during the breeding season, and otherwise the hummingbird simply finds a quiet and unobtrusive place to perch. Depending on the air temperature and the available food supply, they may then doze off into a torpid state, somewhat resembling hibernation. It is rare to see hummingbirds in this state because the site is usually well-hidden, but if they are visible, the tiny birds will be puffed into a feathery ball, conserving heat.

Though their flight speed is often exaggerated they are extremely agile fliers, and both courtship and territorial display rituals centre around repeated, stereotyped flight loops that are species specific, together with individual interactions that are highly variable, spur-of-the-moment affairs.

Hummingbirds can be attracted and fed quite readily by commercial feeders. The ones without a perch are best (it is only hummingbirds that do not need a perch), and the sugar solution can be just that. A 4:1 mix of water with regular table sugar works fine, and is better than the more expensive packages of dyed sugar. Vitamins and proteins come from the insect part of the diet so no supplements are needed. If the birds stop visiting, check for clogged holes in the feeder and ants.

A range of further parallels can be explored:

Because there are fish, there will be birds that specialize on feeding on them.

Because there are flowers, there will be animals (because they are mobile) that pollinate them.

Because there are animals, there will be parasites and predators.

Table 1.3 shows examples of bird species that fill the same roles in the two countries, and Table 1.4 shows a list of common bird species and invertebrate groups. There are more species of birds in the United States (the 810 plus 350 regional forms are nearly twice the numbers found in the UK) and they include more colourful varieties. (The bright yellow finches, warblers and tanagers, the blue jays and scarlet-throated hummingbirds with their shiny metallic green coats immediately come to mind.) Of course exterior coloration describes only a small part of the individual, and codes of truth in advertising must be regarded as variable, at best, as noted below in remarks on poisonous species.

The commonness of flight

Flight itself is a significant common denominator that transcends geographical boundaries rather easily. Fifty-six per cent or so of the described species in the world are insects, most of which fly at some stage in their life cycle, a quarter of the world's mammals are bats, and birds are the most broadly distributed class of vertebrates. (The non-flying human is thus something of an exception in certain statistical measures.) Patterns of flight can be strongly diagnostic.

Table 1.3 Bird species that fill the same roles

UK	USA
Coot	American coot
Sparrowhawk	Red-tailed hawk
Grey heron	Great blue heron
Wood-pigeon	Mourning dove
Green woodpecker	Red-bellied woodpecker
Nuthatch	White-bellied nuthatch
Eurasian jay	Blue jay
	Scrub jay
Crow	American crow

Table 1.4 Animals common to both countries

Bird species

Pheasant	Moorhen
Barn owl	Northern wren
Sand martin	House sparrow
Swallow	Starling
Magpie	

Invertebrates (species may differ)

Dragonflies	Damselflies
Ladybirds	Spittlebugs
Hornets	Spiders
Cockchafer (June bug)	Butterflies and moths
Maybugs	Centipedes and millipedes
Earwigs	Lice, mites, ticks
Fleas	Worms
Bees and wasps	Flies
Slugs and snails	Ants

For example, within the birds:

Sparrows have rapid wing beats and multiple short flights.

Woodpeckers have a dipping flight across fields and through woodland.

Hummingbirds have very visible, high-climbing display flights.

Finches use a bounding flight with wings completely closed at times.

Starlings can be identified through direct paths between stops.

Vultures soar in circular paths without beating their wings.

Flight is extremely efficient in energy use per unit distance, but very costly in energy per unit time. The majority of species that use it tend to do so carefully, and flying for fun is rare. It is possible to keep large and splendid birds of prey in captivity partly because they are quite content to sit still if food is available. So many adaptations to flight are not random but are tied quite closely to the life-history.

Common invertebrates

The long list of common invertebrate groups is quite striking and most readers/gardeners/observers will have no trouble in making mental checkmarks for all of these – the last ones on the list, slugs, snails, flies and ants, perhaps with a rueful nod of the head. The broad distribution of the arthropod invertebrates is likely to be related partly to the early evolution of this phylum. Famously, dragonflies are known to have been around for at least 250 million years. This includes the Triassic and Jurassic ages, and all good dinosaur books seem to show dragonflies on almost every page. The early appearance of arthropods, well before the division into separate continents of the ancient supercontinent of Pangaea, makes it very likely that a large range of groups (classes, orders) are broadly represented. There are two further factors improving the chances of dispersal: the first is the flight capability of the insects, and the second simply derives from being small. Arthropod invertebrates get everywhere, it seems, and today an earwig with a natural home range of perhaps 50 m (164 ft) might have that extended to 9,000 km (5590 miles) – a factor of 180,000 increase! – by stowing away in the suitcase of one of the authors in trips between our respective gardens.

Confusions and curiosities

Sometimes, somewhat artificial differences are magnified or created by different and/or confusing names, and examples are shown in Table 1.5. The theme is repeated for trees and flowering plants in Tables 1.6 and 1.7.

Certain curiosities remain. For example, among the features of American animals not found in the UK is the fact that bats are insectivores in both countries, but only in the United States do some live as nectivores. In Hawaii, there are moth caterpillars that hunt small wasps, crickets and flies and no such terrifying predator is found on either mainland.

Some niches are filled in odd ways. Both hedgehogs and skunks (each unique to the UK and United States, respectively) are killed on roads because they do not run away. In the United States, the armadillo makes an appearance on this sad list.

Continuing the mortal theme, dead bodies must also appear wherever live bodies are expected. Likely dead bodies in the American garden will include those of squirrels, rabbits, mice, chipmunks, armadillos, raccoons, opossums, cats, dogs, birds, snakes, frogs, toads, lizards, spiders, millipedes, insects, worms and more. Reciting the list, we are struck by how infrequently the bodies are encountered and how efficient the natural mopping up process must be.

Poisonous animals and plants

The preferred object of study of four-year-old Conrad Spedding in Los Angeles is the spider, and this is perhaps slightly more hazardous an occupation than it would be in the UK – especially as his avowed favourite is the black widow. We have already noted the more brightly coloured bird species in the United States, and this tendency seems to be mirrored in many other animal species too. There also seems to be a larger number and proportion of poisonous species in the United States, which may signal this with bright colours. (One then also expects this to be more commonly mimicked.) The poison may be delivered by bite (spiders) or sting (wasps), or passively when eaten (various caterpillars). Here, the reason for being poisonous is much the same in plants and animals – to decrease the likelihood of being eaten, and this is not individually much use unless advertised if the predator or herbivore is large compared with its target. Otherwise, small distasteful bites are probably quite effective. Systems have co-evolved with quite specific tastes being harsh or dangerous to one

Table 1.5 Common Names

Different common names for invertebrates (creative differences in description)

UK	USA
Stick insect	Walking stick
Great water beetle	Great water bug
Pond skater	Water strider
Hover-flies	Flower flies
Common wasp	Yellow jacket
Weevils	Snout beetles

Confusing common names

UK	USA
Invertebrates	
Daddy longlegs (for crane flies)	Daddy longlegs (may be used for harvestmen)
Woodlice (they are not lice)	Sowbugs (they are not bugs either)
Birds	
Robin	American robin (a type of thrush)

species but inoffensive or even desirable to others. The chili, for example, would like its fruit to be eaten by birds to distribute the seeds, but not by mammals (why not?), so it contains chemicals that most mammals avoid, but that birds cannot taste.

Human differences

Some points of terminology or custom need clarification. The exhortations to go forth and explore with a torch in Chapter 2 should probably not be taken literally by American residents, who can substitute the word 'flashlight' instead.

Table 1.6 Confusing or equivalent tree names

Common name	UK	USA
Sycamore	*Acer pseudoplatanus* (also occurs in USA)	*Platanus occidentalis* (USA)
Holly	*Ilex aquifolium* (common)	*Ilex opaca* (USA)
Alder	*Alnus glutinosa* (common)	*Alnus rubra* (USA)
Hornbeam	*Carpinus betulus*	*Carpinus caroliniana* (American hornbeam)
Chestnut	*Castanea sativa* (sweet chestnut)	*Castanea dentata* (American chestnut)
Beech	*Fagus sylvatica* (common)	*Fagus grandifolia* (American beech)
Oak	*Quercus robur* (English Oak)	*Quercus alba* (white oak)

Common species

Horse chestnut	*Aesculus hippocastanum*
Lawsons cypress	*Chamaecyparis lawsoniana*
Balsam poplar	*Populus balsamifera*
Sycamore	*Acer pseudoplatanus*

Equivalents

Hawthorn	*Crataegus monogyna* (common)	*Crataegus phaenopyrum* (Washington thorn)
Lime	*Tilia platyphyllos* (common)	*Tilia americana* (American lime)

Table 1.7 Flowering plants

(= denotes common to both countries although local names
may differ; x indicates absence)

UK	USA
Ground ivy	Creeping Charlie
Daisy	English daisy
Oxeye daisy	=
Goldenrod	Meadow goldenrod
Dandelion	=
Shepherd's purse	=
Honesty	=
Bluebell	= (in high western mountains)
Honeysuckle family	
twinflower	=
honeysuckle	x
Elderberry	=
Chickweed	x
Field mouse ear	Meadow chickweed
Bird's foot trefoil	=
Red clover	=
White clover	=
Iris family	= (general)
yellow flag	x
Purple loosestrife	=
Waterlily family	=
Evening primrose	=
Poppy family	
common poppy	Californian poppy
Ribwort plantain	English plantain
Yellow rattle	=

'Dustbin lid' can be quickly translated to 'trash-can lid' but here lies a problem, increasingly shared in the UK, as the old-style cylindrical metal or plastic bin with circular removable lid is replaced by square shapes with hinged lids. The most simple equivalent object in the US might be a pizza box lid. This is at least freely available, broadly distributed, and will probably last quite well in dry conditions. A more sturdy equivalent would be a shallow baking tray, available in just about any supermarket for a dollar or two. Overturned plant pot trays work quite well too, as long as they are opaque.

Crossing the Atlantic

What then, can a book like this offer American readers? Despite the significant differences, and the variation from region to region that makes generalization quite treacherous, we see that the basic principles still apply. There are still more species of insect than any other order, and spiders still astonish us in their numbers and widespread distribution. Larger animals prey on their smaller neighbours. Animals burrow, crawl, scuttle, swim, run, hop, skip, jump, row, flap, soar into, around and out of the plots of land with their porous borders. Flowering plants cross-pollinate courtesy of their roaming insect visitors. Tree branches sway in the wind, and water drops (natural or from sprinklers) come crashing down on the scurrying ants. Common solutions to common physical or biological challenges have evolved. Chlorophyll is green, and camouflage or striking colour codes are arranged accordingly.

That is why we hope a book such as this can travel, whereas a book on plant classification or naming of all types of ground spider does not. We hope that the same sparks can tickle the same pangs of curiosity, and that the book will be both an appetizer and a guide to careful observation, and open-minded questioning. Now there is something worth cultivating.

2 Navigation of the Garden

If, as I suggest, a tour of the garden can be a voyage of discovery, what are the points of the compass that can be used as a guide? It is not sufficient just to wander about hoping to see something interesting: there have to be focusing devices that allow you to get your eye in. This chapter aims, therefore, to illustrate some focal points that can be used for this.

Water

The first focal point is a pond or similar stretch of water in late winter or early spring. Water in the garden is dealt with in detail in Chapter 9, but a pond is used here to make two simple points. Both relate to the fact that most ponds, at this time of year, are full of small crustaceans, especially water fleas *(Daphnia* spp.) and *Cyclops*. These are small creatures (about 1 mm) long but they can easily be seen by the unaided eye, if you are looking for them. They are illustrated in Figure 9.5 but their identifiable characteristics are immediately apparent. *Daphnia* are brown, flattened vertically and proceed in jerks (appearing to hop like fleas), whereas *Cyclops* are whitish and pear-shaped and the females carry a pair of large egg-sacs at the rear end. The two reasons for mentioning this example here are:

(a) that few people expect to see anything at this time of year, as a result of which nothing is spotted unless it is of appreciable size and moves noticeably;

(b) that small creatures that are neither at the surface nor on the bottom are not easily focused upon. The natural tendency is to focus on the surface, the bottom, or substantial intermediate objects, such as weed or fish. Focusing on the water itself is difficult until something has been seen in it and this is unlikely if you do not really think that there is anything there.

As with so many things, once they have been noticed they cannot be missed, probably ever again. The same is true of dust in the air, which may only be revealed by a shaft of sunlight, or cobwebs rendered visible by moisture or sunlight – or sometimes when they are silhouetted.

This general principle, that some things are never seen unless they are looked for and they are never looked for unless it is known that they may be there, goes for all kinds of signs of animal life (as will be evident from other chapters) and also of plant life (especially buds). It is, more surprisingly, also true of animal behavioural signs, which pass unnoticed until they are pointed out. Of course, sometimes – as in the case of small aquatic creatures – it is actually difficult to see them, often because of the nature of the background. The bottom of a pond is generally dark and covered with mud or dead leaves, against which small animals may not show up. The simple insertion of a white surface (tray or board) immediately transforms the scene, especially in terms of numbers.

A bank of flowers

The second focal point is quite different. The flowers have to be appropriate for this purpose, preferably open, radial *Compositae* or *Rosaceae* (for example *Senecio laxifolia* are ideal), loaded with pollen, but buddleia (for example *Buddleja alternifolia*, *B. davidii*) is probably the best-known example. In the late spring or early summer, such a bank of flowers is a place where a wide range of bees, and some other insects, collect pollen. Fine weather helps – sunshine is ideal.

The most visible are the bumble-bees, huge queens in the earlier part of the year, busy collecting pollen to stock the cells in which they lay their eggs. These eggs become the first generation of workers and, later in the season, it is these smaller worker bees that will be seen. Because they are busy, it is relatively easy to observe them. You can even work out which flowers they are likely to visit next – the ones that are most loaded with pollen (usually gold-coloured) as distinct from those where the anthers have gone brown.

Busy is an extremely apt description, both of the way they move from one flower to another and of their behaviour on the flower itself.

It is quite clear what they are doing: they are using their first two pairs of legs to collect the pollen and pack it on to the blobs of pollen usually visible on the hind legs. There they are, right in front of you, scrabbling away, and the pollen-sacs are readily visible. But can you see a leg actually putting pollen on to the sacs?

Of course, the pollen grains are very small (see Box 2.1), so that if you brush your finger on to the anthers a yellow dust can be seen, but no individual grains. This is a pity, since they all have characteristic shapes. They are often sufficiently sticky that the bees do not have to add anything to make the grains stick together, but saliva may also be used. When their pollen sacs are full, the bees depart: this occurs so quickly that it is nearly impossible to say for sure which direction they took.

One soon notices that these bumble-bees vary in colour. Most of them have a dark brown or black background colour, crossed by

---

Box 2.1 Pollen

The function of pollen in the plant is, of course, to fertilize the ovum and thus to generate fertile seed. It is a vital part of sexual reproduction in most flowering plants. The most common – and obvious – pollen feeders are bees, both social and solitary. The adults of these insects have already developed their bodies and can live mainly (but often not entirely) on nectar, which provides soluble carbohydrates. The essential proteins are derived from pollen, which contains 7–30 per cent of protein, varying with plant species. In addition, most pollen contains about 20 per cent water; about 5 per cent fats, oils and waxes; various vitamins; and small quantities of salts of K, P, Ca, Mg and Fe.

The quantities of pollen involved are hard to determine. It has been estimated that a colony of about 200,000 honey-bees would need 23–46 kg (50–100 lb) (= 2–4 million bee loads), mainly to feed to growing grubs and immature workers.

Pollen is produced in enormous quantities and pollen grains are of many different shapes and structures, characteristic of the species. Furthermore, the wall of the pollen grain is virtually indestructible by the normal processes of decay that occur in peat bogs and these 'shells' are usually left in bumble-bee nests in the faeces of the larvae that feed on them. Consequently, it has been found possible to identify the plants growing in an area from the Ice Age onwards by the pollen grains lodged in dateable layers of peat.

---

transverse bands of yellow or silvery-white, but these bands vary in number and position and can be used to identify the species. Tail colour is also important. Some, however, such as the carder-bees (see Box 2.2), are usually tawny-brown without marked bands of colour. With some flowers, the bees are just collecting pollen and not seeking nectar, so their long tongues are not evident.

Box 2.2 Carder-bees

These are really bumble-bees but, whereas the majority of bumble-bees nest in holes in the ground (for example old mouse-holes), carder-bees mostly nest above ground. They construct a covering of grass and moss, often finely interwoven – which is why they are called carder-bees, 'carding' being the old process of combing wool or flax. They tend to do this in long grass, where they are not especially noticeable, but will also utilize covered areas, such as under an upturned bucket or a dustbin lid (see Chapter 11). The nests are usually roughly circular and about 15 cm (6 in) across: the height may be 5–10 cm (2–4 in), depending upon how deep they have penetrated below.

There are three main species:

1. The moss carder-bee (*Bombus muscorum*) is the largest, with the queen measuring about 1.7 cm ($^2/3$ in) long and the workers half this size, coloured orange-brown with yellowish bands on the abdomen.

2. The knapweed carder-bee (*Bombus sylvarum*) is smaller and yellowish-grey with some black and a whitish tail. The name is derived from its fondness for the flower heads of black knapweed (*Centaurea nigra*).

3. The brown-banded carder-bee (*Bombus solstitialis*) is also small (1.5 cm/$^5/8$ in) and mainly yellowish-brown, with some bands of yellow and brown on the abdomen and a black tip to the tail.

In all these species, bees can be seen wandering over the top of the nest day and night, entering it from below via a tunnel in the surrounding grass. If the top of such a nest is gently lifted off, a collection of orange/brown waxen cells can be seen, within which the offspring develop. The bees appear to tolerate such short-term disturbance and are not particularly aggressive: in any case, their numbers are not very great (about 50–100).

In addition to the bumble-bees, of which there are about nine British species, honey-bees will probably be present (although the varroa mite has wiped out many colonies) and a whole range of smaller bees. The latter are solitary bees (see Box 2.3) and are mostly smaller than honey-bees. Some, such as the red osmia (*Osmia rufa*), can easily be distinguished by the fact that they do not collect pollen on the hind legs but spread it uniformly on the underside of the abdomen. Tiny pollen beetles may also be seen, mainly dark brown/black in colour and shiny.

Box 2.3 Solitary bees

These bees, unlike the social bees (for example honey-bees and bumble-bees), do not form colonies and therefore have no 'workers', only males and females. They often appear very early in the spring and pollinate pears and plums in particular. There are a great many different species in Britain, belonging to nine different families (one family alone has about 30 species). The following summary illustrates the range of size, colour and nesting-site, in which individual cells are formed of varying materials and are stocked with honey and/or pollen, in which a single egg is laid.

Common name	Latin name	Length mm*	Markings	Cells made of	Nest site
Common yellow face	*Prosopis communis*	6	black with some yellow on face	liquid from female's mouth – which sets soil	in previous year's stems of bramble and dock
Early morning bee	*Andrena albicans*	11	red/brownish and hairy		15–30 cm deep burrows in soil
Parasitic bee	*Nomada bifida*	8	brown with some yellow on abdomen (often wasp-like)		lays its eggs in burrows of *Andrena* spp.
Blue carpenter	*Ceratina cyanea*	6	metallic blue	bramble pith and saliva	in bramble stems

Common name	Latin name	Length mm*	Markings	Cells made of	Nest site
Patchwork leaf-cutter	*Megachile centuncularis*	10	bright brown and hairy	pieces cut out of rose leaves	mostly in the ground
Mason bee (Red Osmia)	*Osmia rufa*	12	blackish coated with orange hairs	earth plus saliva	holes in walls, rotten wood, soil
Golden rod nomad (cuckoo bee)	*Nomada solidaginis*	8	brownish/ black with some yellow bands on abdomen		parasitic on other bees

* (25 mm = 1 in)

Box 2.4 Solitary wasps

There are only seven species of social wasps in Britain but there are many more species of solitary wasps. As with solitary bees, there are no workers and no colony is ever formed, although many individuals may locate their burrows quite close together. They all provision their cells with small creatures such as insects and spiders which are stung to paralyse them but keep them alive.

The following examples illustrate the main groups.

Group	Example species	Length, mm*	Markings	Nest provision for young	Food
Potter wasp	*Eumenes coarctata*	12	black and yellow	clay 'flask' cemented to heather	caterpillars
Mason wasps (15 spp.)	*Odynerus parietum*	6	black and yellow	burrows in a bank or wall	caterpillars
Ruby-tailed wasps	*Chrysis viridula*	8	shiny blue-black thorax, ruby abdomen	parasitic on mason wasps	

Group	Example species	Length, mm*	Markings	Nest provision for young	Food
Velvet-ants (not really ants)	*Mutila europoea*	12	red and black	parasitic on bumble-bee larvae	
Spider-hunting wasps (17 spp.)	*Pompilus viaticus*	8	black and red	burrows in sand dunes	spiders
Sand wasps	*Sphex sabulosa*	18	black and red	burrows in earth or wood	insects or spiders
Black wasps	*Pemphredon lugubris*	12	black	burrows in posts and stumps	aphids
Digger wasps	*Mellinus arvensis*	12	black and yellow	30–50 cm burrows in soil	flies (other species use spiders, beetles or bees)
Wood-boring wasps	*Trypoxylon figulus*	12	mainly black	holes in wood	spiders

* (25 mm = 1 in)

Wasps are unlikely to visit the bank of flowers, since the adults do not eat or collect pollen and do not usually feed on nectar. The only reason for wasps to visit flowers is to hunt for other insects, on which they feed their grubs (for example the common wasp) or with which they provision their nests (as with most solitary wasps – see Box 2.4).

However, there are other flower masses where insects collect nectar and little pollen is available. This is the case with thyme and cotoneaster, both of which have quite small flowers. This makes it relatively easy to see the remarkable tongues of nectar-feeders. Those of bumble-bees are the longest of the bees (see Box 7.2) but they are greatly exceeded by those of butterflies and moths (see Box 2.5). With larger flowers, especially those with deep corollas, the front part of the insect disappears and the tongue cannot be seen.

Box 2.5 Tongues of butterflies and moths

Of all the insects, butterflies and moths have the longest tongues. This means that they can obtain nectar from very deep flowers which even bumble-bees cannot reach.

The typical insect mouthparts have been modified so that two parts are immensely elongated and form a tube, the sides being held together by hooks. This long tube, or proboscis, is coiled like a watch spring under the head when not in use and extended for sucking up nectar.

The length is very variable but in the tortoiseshell butterfly, for example, may commonly be 14 mm (just over $^1/2$ in).

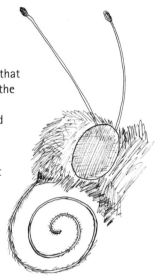

Head of a butterfly showing the coiled tongue

All these features can be seen just by observing one kind of site, a bank or mass of flowers. The same is true for some wild flowers. For example, the *Umbelliferae* (such as hedge parsley, wild carrot and cow parsnip) seem to be favoured by a whole range of beetles (for example the soldier-beetle, *Rhagorycha fulva*) and hover-flies, especially the drone-fly *Eristalis tenax* (see Box 2.6).

Box 2.6 Hover-flies

This is another very diverse group: 85 different species were recorded in one suburban garden over a period of eight years. Unfortunately very few have common names, but most can be identified by their colour patterns, which are often bright.

Many of the common ones look superficially like wasps. In the air, they hover and can fly backwards and even sideways. At rest, they can be distinguished from bees and wasps because, being true flies (Order *Diptera*), they only have one pair of wings. As with crane-flies, the hind pair of wings is represented by club-shaped balancers or halteres (see Box 7.7). Like all fast fliers, they have large eyes and huge thoracic muscles which, like those of bumble-bees, can be put out of gear with the wings and used to heat up the body.

They are all completely harmless and most are useful: many of them feed on aphids (those of the sub-family *Syrphinae*) and can eat up to 1200 aphids during the course of development. Adults mostly feed on nectar and pollen (and are useful pollinators of onions, carrots and fruit trees, for example) and it is the larvae that feed voraciously on aphids, although the larvae of some species scavenge in decaying matter, some live on plant tissues and others live in the nests of social insects (bees, wasps and ants).

The major causes of death among adults are parasitism, fungal disease and being eaten by wasps (social and solitary), dungflies, birds (such as fly-catchers) and spiders. Mating occurs mainly in flight and the eggs are laid near to the larval food source.

Some specialized hover-flies have rather different life-styles. A common example is the drone-fly (*Eristalis tenax*), which lays its eggs in rotting carcasses, drains, rotting matter, sewage or stagnant water. The larvae are adapted to this mode of life by having a long, telescopic 'tail' (which may be four or five times as long as the body, which itself may be up to 1 cm [^{1}/2 in] long): this functions as a breathing-tube so that the larvae can obtain oxygen while living in anaerobic conditions. These larvae are often called (understandably) 'rat-tailed maggots'.

Identifying species by their behaviour was mentioned in Chapter 1 and a good example of this is to be seen on buddleia (*Buddleja* spp.), in the shape of the day-flying silver Y moth (*Plusia gamma*), which keeps its wings moving in a grey blur, nearly all the time. Just occasionally, the characteristic Y marking can be seen. It is mainly in the UK as a summer migrant from southern Europe.

A sunny wall

In the late spring and early summer, a sunny wall is used by all kinds of insects to warm up, though, strangely enough, this does not usually include spectacular insects such as butterflies. These, of course, would be noticed anyway and the reason for using a wall as this example is precisely because you do not expect to see anything and would probably regard it as not worth looking at.

In fact, some interesting insects rest there in the sun and, because of that, certain spiders live there in order to hunt them. The zebra spider (see page 22) is a common example, its black and white stripes making it easy to identify. It is quite small, with shortish legs, so it is not as off-putting as other spiders to those who cannot really stand them (and we all tend to have some phobias – snakes, slugs, worms and so on). Related to the spiders are the mites and the small, red velvet mites can often be seen scuttling across walls.

The zebra spider does not spin a web but catches its prey with a short dash at it. It lives in crevices in the brickwork or around window-sills, so, in common with most wall-dwellers, it is more usually found on old walls.

Old houses, with plenty of cracks in the brickwork, mortar or woodwork, harbour an additional range of creatures, especially solitary bees and wasps (see Boxes 2.3 and 2.4). These may be observed coming and going and do no real harm. Although solitary, with each female provisioning its own tunnelful of cells, they often nest in groups – perhaps a step in the direction of forming a social colony.

The bees are generally more furry than the wasps and the latter mostly have brighter colours, rather like the common wasp but on a much smaller scale. The bees can be seen carrying in loads of pollen, very often on the underside of the abdomen and not on the hind legs, as bumble-bees and honey-bees do.

The solitary wasps, on the other hand, all provision their cells with paralysed (but still living) prey, sometimes almost as big as themselves. Each species of wasp sticks to one sort of prey species – a spider, a caterpillar, a bee and so on.

Wherever these solitary bees and wasps nest, there are also almost certain to be their parasites, usually other wasps that sit in wait until their hosts have laid an egg in the tunnel and are away, when they nip in and lay their own egg which will eventually produce a grub that consumes the original occupant. One of these is the ruby-tailed wasp (*Chrysis cyanea*), with a shiny metallic body, the abdomen being the colour of a ruby. Actually, there are several species, of very different sizes, up to 1 cm (1/2 in), but the group is easily distinguished once seen.

A brick path

A situation very similar to that of the wall presents itself on a path. Like a wall, an old path is more interesting because it is likely to have more cracks and crevices, and it is in these that small creatures have their homes. The most common signs are small holes and little heaps of earth, made up of small grains or particles.

A scattering of soil and tiny openings usually indicate small black ants (*Lasius niger*) and these may occur over quite a long season. Periodically, the winged queens emerge to go on their mating flight, appearing in their hundreds. Larger, perfectly circular holes usually indicate solitary bees or wasps: these can be distinguished by their appearance. The most common of the burrowing bees are *Andrena* spp., furry little bees of varying sizes but smaller than a honey bee. The most frequently occurring digger wasps are striped in black and yellow and are not hairy. As with the wall surface, parasitic bees and wasps may lie in wait to take advantage of the owner's absence.

Brick and bare earth paths provide much the same habitat. Grass paths may also be used but holes are really quite difficult to see in even very short grass. All these surfaces tend to show most activity on warm, sunny days, but night-time has its own fauna.

Exploring with a torch

Walking round your garden after dark usually brings to your attention night-scented flowers such as honeysuckle or stock and bats that can be seen flitting against the sky. Without the torch, it is remarkable how pale flowers stand out, as do some paving stones and quite unexpected features such as dandelion seed heads which, in numbers, look like little lanterns.

However, a torch reveals many other creatures. Warm moist evenings show most activity on the ground, with an astonishing number of earthworms on a lawn, slugs and snails pursuing their slow path and the occasional pair of illuminated eyes of a mammal such as a fox. In some ways, however, the area of the garden which reveals most at night is a pond. Usually, a large part of the problem of seeing anything in a pond is the tremendous reflection of daylight (and sunlight especially) from the surface. You can often see much more of your own reflection and that of sky or overhanging trees than you can of the inhabitants. In the dark, there is none of this and the beam of a torch picks out all the nocturnally active creatures: newts, crustaceans, frogs and toads in the spring, diving beetles and their larvae and dragonfly nymphs. (Nymphs are the early stages of insects that gradually develop and emerge, while larvae are the early stages of those insects that form pupae within which the whole body is reorganized to emerge as a quite different-looking adult.) Most of these creatures are largely nocturnal but do not seem greatly bothered by torchlight. More details about water at night are given in Chapter 9.

Pigeons and ducks will fly off if disturbed in the dark but only rarely does one see where common birds spend the night. Many insects also fly at night, mosquitoes, gnats and midges being the most annoying, the females seeking a meal of (mostly mammalian) blood. Other insects are active, some of them in our interests, such as hover-fly larvae eating aphids, and for this reason bats are also nocturnal, since there are then fewer aerial predators and bats do not depend upon sight to navigate or catch their prey.

The night also has characteristic sounds, the most obvious being the hooting of owls and the barking of foxes, both most noticeable in autumn and early winter, and the croaking of frogs for a short time in the spring. Some birds sing after dark, including the nightingale and the blackcap, but the only bird activity that is truly nocturnal is the hunting of owls.

Damaged vegetation

Whether your first thought on seeing damaged foliage is to destroy the leaf and the culprit (preferably in one go) or to wonder what interesting activity is going on, it is worth knowing what is responsible. Curative or preventive measures may be indicated but sometimes they may be unnecessary or even undesirable. Five types of damage stand out: (i) holes eaten in the leaf; (ii) a crumpled leaf; (iii) a discoloured leaf; (iv) a leaf with warty growths: (v) tunnels in the leaf.

Holes

Some holes appear in the middle of leaves, while some are cut out at the edges. A wide range of insects cause such holes (see Table 2.1), some eating the leaf tissue, others using it as a protective shield and yet others removing the excised piece to line a nest.

Table 2.1 Holes in leaves

Insect species	Nature of the hole
Leaf-cutter bee (*Megachile centuncularis*)	Almost circular pieces cut out of the edge of the leaf
Cockchafer (*Melolantha melolantha*)	Irregular areas removed from leaf margin
Pea and bean weevils (*Sitona* spp.)	Notched edges of leaves
Leaf beetles (*Donacia* spp.), larvae of the leek moth (*Acrolepia assectella*) and the mustard beetle (*Phaedon cochleariae*)	Holes within the leaf area
Colorado beetle (*Leptinotarsa decemlineata*) and larvae of cabbage white butterfly (*Pierisrapae*)	Indiscriminate damage – even skeletonizing the leaf

Holes made in rose leaves by leaf-cutter bees

Crumpled leaves

Sometimes crumpled leaves are caused by bacterial or fungal disease and quite often they result from massive aphid attack. When leaves are folded back on themselves (or sometimes stuck together), it will usually be found that they are 'sewn' together with silken threads to form a capsule within which a caterpillar or grub makes its home. It is thus protected to some extent and, in any case, is less visible, except, of course, for the fact that to humans – and perhaps to birds as well – the folded leaf actually gives it away and you don't have to look under every leaf to find the animal.

In some cases a silken cocoon is woven on the under surface of the leaf, and may not cause marked folding or curling. Within this a caterpillar may lurk or, just as likely, a spider guarding its eggs. Even if the spider cannot be seen, the egg mass may be visible through the side of the cocoon.

Discoloured leaves

These can be caused by disease or nutritional disorders: mineral deficiencies are often indicated by particular colour changes. Just as nitrogen supply affects the colour of grass – heavy nitrogen applications producing a deep green (sometimes blueish) colour – a shortage of nitrogen results in yellowing of the leaf.

Leaves with warty growths

Such growths exhibit an extraordinary variety, in size, shape and colour. Most commonly they are caused by a parasite, very often a midge or a parasitic wasp, and often a very small one. When a wasp lays its egg in the tissue of the leaf, the plant isolates it by surrounding it with a proliferation of cells. This forms the growth, usually in the form of a gall. If a sizeable gall is cut open, the grub can be seen in the centre. There are many different gall wasps and many different and characteristic galls (see Table 2.2 and Box 7.5).

Table 2.2 Examples of plant galls caused by gall wasps

(86% of gall wasp species induce galls on oak trees)

Wasp species	Nature of gall
Diplolepis rosae	Bedeguar on wild roses
Biorhiza pallida	Spherical 'oak apple'
Neuroterus lenticularis	'Spangle' galls on underside of oak leaves
Andricus kollari	Spherical marble gall on young oaks

When the egg hatches, the developing grub feeds on the tissue of the gall and thus enlarges the chamber in which it is enclosed, eventually emerging through a hole it makes. Clearly this part of the life-cycle has to be completed before the leaf withers and decays. However, many galls (such as those listed in Table 2.2) are not actually part of a leaf or stem and commonly survive (in a dried form) long after leaves have fallen.

Tunnels in the leaf

Tunnels are made between the two surfaces of leaves (that is, between the two epidermal layers) and cause the affected area to lose colour, showing up as pale wriggly lines. They may be caused by the larvae of many creatures, including those of very small moths. An example of the latter is the lilac leaf-miner (larvae of the moth *Gracilaria syringella*). These tiny caterpillars often operate as a group and cause such damage that the leaf goes brown and crumpled. The larvae then make it into a funnel-like shelter and feed on the outside of the leaf.

Compass points

This chapter started with the idea of using specific sites as 'compass points' in navigating the garden in order to 'get one's eye in'. This is particularly helpful in showing other people, especially children, because the chances of seeing something interesting are thereby increased. However, once you have got your eye in, you are not restricted to these sites and you begin to look at everything in the same way. You even wander over the lawn with an eye to little holes or disturbances. In short, you see the world differently.

3 Plants in the Garden

For the most part, the plants in the garden are there because we put them there – or at least tolerate them. This is quite different from garden animals (see Chapter 4), hardly any of which do we introduce and most of which we are completely unaware of. Furthermore, plants stay put, unless they die. They are individually immobile, in the sense that they are, literally, rooted to the spot, which does not, of course, mean that they cannot move their leaves and shoots or distribute seed.

Unlike many animals, plants tend to seek the light and many seek prominence over the plants around them. They vary in the amount of light, especially direct sunlight, that they favour and some only thrive in shady places. In fact, a wide variety of plants are regarded as shade-loving, for example ransomes, wood anemones, bluebells, ferns, lily of the valley, hellebore, solomon's seal, alchemilla and pulmonaria. But most, except fungi and parasitic plants, live and grow by photosynthesis (see Box 3.1). They also vary in their preferences for soil pH, soil moisture, ambient temperature (winter and summer), including tolerance of frost, and exposure to wind. Gardeners are only too well aware of all these factors and spend considerable time and ingenuity in selecting plants and sites that match their needs.

Other plants occur as weeds (see Box 3.2), although many of them may be both beautiful and interesting. A few gardeners may actually cultivate such weeds and may even sow some areas with wild flowers, but these tend to be in isolated parts of the garden; there may be the odd patch of nettles (for the butterflies, you know!) or rough grass between the fruit trees, or grass verges that contain many unplanned species. However, the essence of most gardening is a controlled array of plants, chosen mostly for their appearance, sometimes for their scent (for example lilac, lilies, lavender, roses, sweet rocket and pinks), and occasionally for their contributions to privacy and shelter. Vegetable gardening and the growing of tree fruits are quite different, intended to produce useful, valuable, wanted products, but the characteristics of control, over species and growth, are the same.

Box 3.1 Photosynthesis

Photosynthesis is the process by which green plants absorb sunlight (in the 0.4–0.7 mm wavelength region of the spectrum, which includes rather less than half the total solar radiation) and use the energy liberated to produce sugars and carbohydrates, proteins, fatty acids, fats and a variety of other compounds. The mechanism for absorbing light is the green system of plastids, which contain the chlorophyll.

The light intensity on a clear day is often some four times what a leaf needs to operate at its maximum level of carbohydrate production. There is thus, at these times, more solar energy being received than large, horizontally displayed leaves can use. That is why many plants thrive with overlapping layers of leaves (as in trees) or with near-vertical leaves (as in grasses).

Box 3.2 Weeds

Most garden weeds depend on human activity to provide suitable conditions to grow – open space, fertile soil and often moisture. If a garden was abandoned, the garden weeds would probably be displaced within a few years.

Garden weeds are often specialists at colonizing disturbed soil (because their seeds require exposure to bright light in order to germinate) but their seeds survive for long periods in undisturbed soil – far longer than the seeds of cultivated plants. Dock (for example *Rumex obtusifolius*) seeds can lie dormant for 100 years and a single plant of fat hen (*Chenopodium album*) can produce 70,000 seeds in one year. The stores of buried weed seeds in the soil can be very large indeed – often in the order of 5,000–10,000 viable weed seeds per m^2 (sq yd) – so effective weed control should always include the prevention of seeding.

Some weeds, however, survive by reproducing vegetatively (from bits of root, for example) and many have roots and rhizomes that contain massive food reserves. Many weeds have much more extensive root systems than cultivated plants and thus survive better in adverse conditions (such as drought). This is spectacularly illustrated by common weeds such as goose-grass or cleavers (*Galium aparine*) and herb robert (*Geranium robertianum*), both of which have extensive root systems (albeit easily uprooted) connected to the plant by a remarkably narrow single stem, from which all the leaves spring. Some weeds have deep tap roots (for example the dandelion, *Taraxacum Sect. vulgaria*) and others develop from rhizomes (for example white bryony, *Bryonia cretica*).

These features have evolved because they assist in the survival of the plants. Most weeds have not been selected for large flower size or colour, but some flowers are as large as the cultivated equivalents (for example the field bindweed, *Convolvulus arvensis*, or, even larger, the hedge bindweed, *Calystegia sepium*).

It is worth considering the inclusion of certain 'weeds' into a garden – or, perhaps more accurately, tolerating them, since they usually arrive unaided! The geraniums are good examples. Quite different from the relatively tender pelargoniums (with which they shared the name 'geranium' from 1732, for about 200 years). The names refer to the beak-like seed capsule (for example cranesbill, storksbill) and geranium comes from the Greek geranos – a crane. Herb robert (*Geranium robertianum*) grows anywhere but is easily removed after flowering: other species and crosses are larger and more spectacular, however.

In some countries, plants are grown for their medicinal qualities. For example, in China, gingko is thought to aid artery recovery and in India coriander seeds are used to reduce inflammation. Other medicinal plants and their claimed uses are: thyme (antiseptic), lungwort (for coughs), nasturtium (to aid digestion), milk thistle seeds (for liver regeneration) and sage (antiseptic). We need to be careful about dismissing 'old-wives tales'. Tansy, for example, is an effective insecticide and will keep away fleas, wasps and even rats, so its reputation for protecting against the plague (spread by rats and fleas) may not have been undeserved.

Since all these plants are chosen for the garden, their species, Latin names and characteristic features are usually known. Less tends to be known about their physiology and growth, their nutrition and, apart from the practical needs of gardening, their reproduction.

Physiology

A group of students, when asked what a tree trunk was made of and where its constituents came from, replied that it all came from the roots and thus consisted of whatever was taken up by them! In fact, a tree trunk, as with most plants, mainly consists (apart from water) of carbon, in the form of carbohydrates, such as cellulose, hemi-cellulose and lignin – none of them taken up by the roots but all the products of photosynthesis. Green leaves, buds and stems also contain minerals and nitrogenous compounds, such as protein.

The minerals taken up by the roots, all dissolved in water, represent only a minor part of the plant, however (see Table 3.1), and nitrogen is also a small constituent. It is worth remembering that whatever the form of fertilizer or manure that is applied, what the plant can actually take up through the roots has to be soluble in water. The water itself is physiologically vital; it transports nutrients and metabolic products and it provides the turgor of cells that allows plants to retain their shape. This latter point is well illustrated by the wilting of plants when they have insufficient water.

Table 3.1 Mineral composition of the plant

This varies with species and stage of growth but the range and magnitude of the nutrients required can be illustrated by their presence in the plant. The following table shows the mineral composition of two major herbage species, perennial ryegrass and white clover, chosen as examples because the data are available for such agricultural crops. These species also occur in gardens.

Mineral	Ryegrass % in dry matter (or ppm* where stated)	White Clover % in dry matter (or ppm* where stated)
Phosphorus	0.26–0.42	0.25–0.40
Potassium	1.98–2.50	2.09–3.11
Calcium	0.4–1.0	1.36–2.10
Magnesium	0.09–0.25	0.18–0.24
Sulphur	0.13–0.75	0.24–0.36
Sodium	0.10–0.57	0.12–0.41
Chlorine	0.39–1.30	0.62–0.91
Iron	50–200 ppm	117–291 ppm
Manganese	22–200 ppm	51–87 ppm

Mineral	Ryegrass % in dry matter (or ppm* where stated)	White Clover % in dry matter (or ppm* where stated)
Zinc	15–60 ppm	25–29ppm
Copper	5.4–8.5 ppm	7.3–8.7ppm
Cobalt	0.15–0.16 ppm	0.13–0.24ppm
Iodine	0.22–1.45 ppm	0.14–0.44ppm
Selenium	0.1–1.0 ppm	0.005–153ppm
Lead**	0.3–3.5 ppm	0.3–3.5ppm
Silica	0.6–1.2	0.03–0.12

*Parts per million

**This illustrates the fact that composition may not always reflect need but sometimes external contamination.

The remarkable capacity for water to provide the pressures that keep stems erect is well shown in hippeastrum and dandelion flower stems. These are hollow and, if the ends are deeply split, the sides curve outwards (see Figure 3.1) and bend up because of the outward pressure they are under (this is the same property that allows spring onions to be turned into decorative sprays).

Figure 3.1 Dandelion
sides of slit stem curling back

Water has other important functions. The flow of soluble nutrients depends upon water being evaporated from the leaves (through very small holes, called stomata – see Box 3.3) and the rate of this is governed by the temperature and humidity of the air. This evaporation

Box 3.3 Stomata

Stomata are very small pores in the leaf epidermis, through which water vapour escapes and exchange of gases (CO_2, O_2) takes place. They are very small (about 15 µm – 35 µm) and very numerous, with some 10,000 per cm^2 ($^1/_2$ sq in).

They are surrounded by 'guard' cells, which can close the aperture and thus reduce water loss: this happens markedly when the plant wilts but operates continuously to control the rate of evaporation.

Plants adapted to dry conditions often have rolled leaves with the stomata on the inside surface.

---

process also cools the leaves and prevents overheating. Notice how cool growing grass can feel, even on a hot day, to bare feet.

All this requires a good water supply from the soil and the water-collecting capacity of roots depends on their surface area: most plants have a large network of very fine roots and the surface area is greatly increased by the fine root hairs that occur near the root-tip, just behind the zone of active root growth. These root hairs can only function when they are in close contact with moisture-bearing surfaces and this is a very delicate relationship (often disrupted in transplanting, which is why one waters them in). On the other hand, roots need oxygen (in most plants) and, apart from bog and aquatic plants, waterlogging prevents this being met.

If all these (and more) physiological functions are working satisfactorily and the ambient temperature is adequate, growth occurs. Although the radiant energy of sunlight (which does not have to be direct) is needed for photosynthesis, and growth will not be able to occur if photosynthesis is prevented, extension growth may also occur in the dark.

Growth

Growth is quite difficult to define. Increase in size, weight and length are all used to measure growth but do you consider that you have grown if you put on weight? Different parts of the plant can grow at different rates and most growth is accompanied by 'development' or an increase in complexity.

In a sense, we all know what we mean by it, but it is worth distinguishing, for example, between an increase in the number of cells and their expansion due to an intake of water. A good example is provided by the buds of trees. We tend to think of these buds as features of the spring but, in fact, most of them are formed in early winter. They are relatively small, full of tiny, closely packed cells with little water (and thus relatively resistant to freezing). In the warmer weather of spring-time, these buds suddenly open and leaves burst out to grow rapidly – mainly by expansion of the existing cells with water. Spectacular growth of leaves and shoots is often of this form – purely by extension of what was already there.

Some very rapid growth depends upon stored nutrients, in bulbs, corms, rhizomes and swollen roots. This enables a plant to expand a leafy structure very rapidly, which then provides a large photosynthetic area that powers further growth. Such plants are thus able to compete successfully with others. Others apparently manage without stored reserves. Common cleaver (*Galium aparine*) is a very noticeable example, growing at a tremendous rate, with many clinging stems springing from one very thin stem linked to a large network of fine roots.

Successful weeds are often characterized by very fast, early growth which smothers everything else. Sometimes, attractive plants can be selected that use these same tactics on weeds: rapidly spreading clumps of lungwort (*Pulmonaria* spp.) can even be used to crowd out established nettles (see pages 172-3).

Nutrition

Competition for light may be linked to competition for nutrients. Apart from carbohydrates which can be totally derived from carbon, oxygen and hydrogen – all obtained by gaseous exchanges through the leaves and water via the roots – all the minerals come from the soil, including nitrogen, the element that often dominates growth rate, unless the plant is associated with nitrogen-fixing bacteria (see

Box 3.4). The commonest examples of this are the legumes – peas, beans, clover, vetches, sweet-peas – which have nodules containing bacteria on their roots.

In agriculture, inputs of nitrogenous fertilizer are a major influence on growth and production. In gardens, nitrogen is not necessarily of the same importance quantitatively. Qualitatively, all plants must have nitrogen – it is needed to make protein, for example – but many plants only thrive on soils with a low nitrogen content.

Nitrogen certainly makes grass grow but the finer lawn grasses may need relatively little.

Box 3.4 Nitrogen fixation

Nitrogen (N) is an abundant (about 80 per cent of the atmosphere) but nearly inert gas, consisting of molecules with two atoms each (hence N_2). In biological fixation, ammonia is the initial product. This is only done by bacteria possessing the enzyme nitrogenase, but these are found in a variety of sites. Some of the best known, and agriculturally important, are bacteria of the genus *Rhizobium*, which includes those found in the legumes (such as soya beans, peanuts, peas, beans, clover), where they inhabit nodules on the roots.

These nodules are packed with nitrogen-fixing bacteria (the species varies with the species of plant) and the nitrogen is released directly to the plant, where most of it is formed into proteins, or indirectly to the soil, following death of the root.

Non-leguminous plants (such as the alder tree and the aquatic fern *Azolla*) also contain nitrogen-fixing bacteria and there are many independent, free-living bacteria that can fix nitrogen.

Reproduction

Plants employ a variety of means to reproduce themselves. Some will regenerate from small pieces of root – weeds seem especially good at this (especially couch grass – *Agropyron repens*). Others regularly come up again and again from bulbs, corms, rootstocks and rhizomes. Many spread across the ground by creeping stems (stolons, as in clover) or by runners, for example strawberry. Wild strawberry spreads at an astonishing rate, even in apparently inhospitable areas; every year I am able to transplant new individual plants of wild strawberry from the bricked-over area by my front door, formed wherever their runners find a tiny piece of soil or sand.

Many plants just increase the size of the clump, which can be split as required. Most plants will produce seed, but many garden plants are not allowed to do so, in order to avoid diversion of nutrients to seed that is not actually wanted. Roses, daffodils and lilies are examples, though sometimes rose hips are retained for their colour.

Some, of course, are allowed to self-seed and a great many plants are always produced from seed. Seed size shows enormous variation: small seeds are usually very numerous, thus increasing the chances of a proportion surviving; large seeds are fewer but each seedling is better stocked with reserves of nutrients. Numbers of seeds can be extraordinary: a poppy can contain as many as 17,000 seeds in one head.

Seeds are major methods of survival and dispersal, and again, weeds are often very good at both. As is well known, under dry conditions, some seeds can survive in the soil for hundreds or even thousands of years. They may require some stimulus to cause germination, such as exposure to light or low temperatures, without which they remain dormant. That is why the flora of recently disturbed land is often so spectacular, the disturbance triggering mass germination, for example in poppies. While in the soil, seeds may be eaten by small organisms, including earthworms, although in this case they may be passed through the digestive system undamaged and proceed to germinate. Indeed, odd little flora may be created around earthworm casts where their seeds are concentrated.

The mechanisms that have evolved to aid seed dispersal are very varied and show some of the ways in which plants can achieve movement. Some of it is passive, simply floating on the wind (for example dandelions), or sticking to passing animals by virtue of curved hooks (for example cleavers, burdock), or being eaten in the form of fruit (by birds, for example) with the seed passing through unharmed (for example mistletoe). But there are also spring-loaded mechanisms which actually fling the seed for some distance (see Box 3.5).

Box 3.5 Seed dispersal

There are four main methods of seed dispersal: wind, water, mechanical means and animal transport.

A variety of structures have evolved to assist wind dispersal, for example 'wings' on sycamore seeds, 'parachutes' on dandelions and tree branches adapted to sway in the wind.

Water transport is only really effective in running water and requires sufficient buoyancy, for example seeds of yellow iris (yellow flag) and several water lilies (yellow and white).

Mechanical methods depend mainly on spring-loaded devices usually triggered by drying out of the tissues, for example storksbill and cranesbill (see below).

Animal transport includes seeds that stick or hook onto animal coats (such as burdock and cleavers), seeds excreted after eating of fruit, especially by birds (for example yew berries, hawthorn berries) and aquatic seeds sticking to the feet or plumage of birds (for example bur-reed, water crow-foot).

Bloody cranesbill

seedheads after flowering

spring mechanism for throwing the seed

seeds in position

When seeds germinate, usually involving the absorption of a lot of water, the first growth to emerge is the radicle or root and this often penetrates a remarkable distance down into the soil. Oak seedlings are a good example (burying by squirrels or jays is another means of dispersal). Even quite a small oak seedling will be found to have a tap root going down over 15 cm (6 in).

The first shoot from the seedling grows upwards and may initially bear leaves that are quite different from those associated with the grown plant (see Figure 1.1), but, even later on, many plants have leaves that differ between the upper and lower parts of the plant.

In order to produce seed, the plant must first flower and the flowers have to be pollinated.

Flowers

Many garden plants have been selected for their flower-size and colour and, except for fruit or vegetable production, pollination is unimportant. But large, colourful flowers mainly evolved in order to attract pollinators: those that are wind pollinated are usually much less spectacular. The latter are sometimes specialized, for example, with small female flowers bearing the stigma and large male catkins, bearing many stamens, hanging in the wind (for example hazel, oak). Quite often the shape of the flower determines who can pollinate it. Pollination is further discussed in Boxes 3.6 and 3.7

Box 3.6 Pollination (see also Boxes 3.7, 7.1 and 7.2)

Some flowers are self-fertile; others require cross-pollination between different plants, sometimes with plants of separate sexes. The transfer of pollen from the anthers to the stigma can be effected by wind (anemophilous), insects and other invertebrates.

Wind
Anemophilous plants usually have inconspicuous flowers and the pollen is light, dusty and produced in large quantities. Typical examples are hazel (with catkins), grasses, sedges, rushes, stinging nettles and plantains.

Insects

The most effective pollinators for most garden flowers are bees – honey-bees, bumble-bees and solitary bees. Certain types of flowers (for example *Antirrhinum* spp. and *Aconitum* spp.) are especially favoured by bumble-bees (they are even sometimes known as 'bumble-bee flowers'). In fact, there seems to be a general preference of honey-bees for radially symmetrical flowers and of bumble-bees for those that are irregularly shaped.

Bees are attracted by flower colour (but are red-blind) as well as shape and scent (bees can smell flowers that we cannot, for example toadflax, *Linaria vulgaris*). Flowers often have markings, called nectar-guides, that help a bee to find the nectar and, in so doing, get dusted with pollen. Even inconspicuous flowers (for example those of *Cotoneaster*) are often visited by bumble-bees: it is ultimately the supply of nectar and pollen that determine attractiveness – the other features are simply signals and identification markers. Butterflies seem to be attracted mainly by flowers that are purple (for example *Buddleja*), yellow or orange and red (for example goldenrod, *Solidago*).

For pollinating cross-pollinating fruit trees, bumble-bees are often the most effective since they wander about more and work faster, for longer hours, and in more inclement weather. They also work at lower temperatures than honey-bees and thus (especially the queens) are about earlier in the season. The only problem is their sheer numbers: colonies of honey-bees contain vastly more individuals. The planting of early-flowering plants (for example yellow archangel, *Lamium galobdolon*) has been suggested to provide better foraging for the queens.

Other invertebrates

Other invertebrates also pollinate flowers by carrying pollen that brushes off on them while they are feeding, but only those that fly are likely to have much effect. Flies, ichneumon flies, beetles and wasps are often involved. Some of the mechanisms involved are astonishing (see Box 3.7).

From a gardener's point of view, flowers have two main qualities: they are attractive to look at and, in many cases, they have an attractive scent (also usually evolved to attract insects, often moths, which fly at night), for example honeysuckle, tobacco plants, night-scented stock, lavender, limes, evening primrose, lilies. If they are pollinated by insects, flowers are designed to be attractive to them too, although their perception of them may be quite different from ours. Flowers also provide food for a variety of creatures and a habitat for some very small ones.

Box 3.7 Pollination of the common fig *(Ficus carica)*

The fig tree is well-known, as are its deeply lobed, large, leathery leaves and its globe-shaped fruit. This fruit is actually a swollen flowering and fruiting stem and the visible part is the outside of a cup-shaped flower head, the edges of which are bent over so that they almost meet, leaving a small round hole at the tip. The inside is hollow and the central space is lined with flowers – female at the base and male near the round hole (see below right). A species of gall-wasp (*Blastophaga psenes*) breeds among the female flowers but to reach them or to get to another fig it has to pass the male flowers near the entrance hole, where it gets dusted with pollen. This it transfers to the female flowers, which then develop fruits holding seeds.

Some figs, however, including the Adriatic fig, can ripen without fertilization (called parthenocarpy – self-fertilization is called parthenogenesis).

A similar structure occurs in lords and ladies (*Arum maculatum*) — see below. Insects (for example midges) are attracted by the foetid smell to enter the enclosed flower sheath and are trapped by the down-curving hairs. The flies, which may be covered by pollen from another plant, crawl over – and fertilize – the female flowers. As the lower hairs

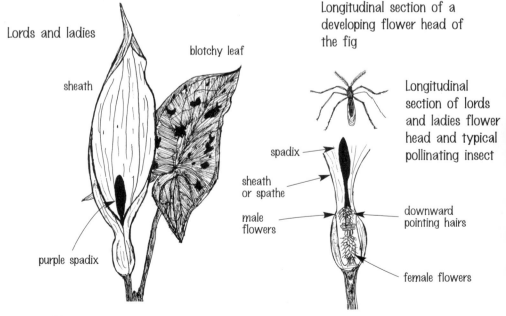

Lords and ladies

blotchy leaf

sheath

purple spadix

Longitudinal section of a developing flower head of the fig

Longitudinal section of lords and ladies flower head and typical pollinating insect

spadix

sheath or spathe

male flowers

downward pointing hairs

female flowers

wither, the flies crawl up to the now mature male flowers and get covered in pollen. Finally the upper hairs wither and the insect escapes: it cannot avoid carrying the pollen from the male flowers of one plant to the female flowers of another. Eventually, bright orange berries are produced.

The food is mainly in the form of nectar (sought by bees, butterflies and moths), pollen (sought by bees of all kinds – social and solitary – and eaten by pollen beetles) and, fortunately, to a lesser extent, petals. Examples of cultivated flowers that attract butterflies are:

Early season   polyanthus, aubretia
Mid-season   honesty
Late season   buddleia, lavender, thyme, ice plants.

Moths are attracted to tobacco plants and ivy flowers. Table 3.2 lists some of the common inhabitants of and visitors to flowers.

Table 3.2 Inhabitants of flowers (and their visitors)

Inhabitants	Activity
Pollen beetles (*Meligethes aeneus*)	feeding on pollen and flowers
Earwigs (*Forficula auricularia*)	usually just hiding
Clover weevil (*Apion apricans*)	larvae eating the ovules
Pea midge (*Contarinia pisi*)	larvae feeding on flowers and pods of peas and beans

Visitors	Activity
Butterflies	seeking nectar
Moths	seeking nectar
Bees	collecting both nectar and pollen
Wasps	seeking nectar
Flies (esp. drone-flies)	seeking nectar

Cultivated flowers, however, which have been developed for their size and colour, may be very poor producers of nectar. Some flowers only open in sunshine: the winter aconite (*Ezanthis hyemalis*) is an example: many close up at night (for example water lily).

There are, or course, many plants that do not have flowers (see Table 3.3) but only the ferns feature prominently in gardens. Their

Table 3.3 Flowerless plants

Main groups	Examples	Habitat
Ferns	*Osmunda regalis*	Wet places
	Dryopteris filix-mas	Wooded areas
	Asplenium spp.	Walls
Fungi	*Nolanea sericea*	Lawns
	Agaricus silvicola	Woodland
	Polyparus squamosus	Bracket fungus on oak, maple etc
	Marasmius ramealis	Dead twigs of brambles or wild roses
	Lycoperdon perlatum	Puffball – on stumps
Lichens	*Lecarnora calcarea*	Walls
	Ramalina calicaris	Trees
Mosses	*Cirriphyllum piliferum*	Grassy places
	Dicranella heteromalla	Everywhere except chalky sites
Liverworts	*Calypoglia muelleriana*	Damp rocks
	Marchanta polymorpha	Marshy places
	Lunularia cruciata	Gardens and greenhouses
Stoneworts	*Chara hispada*	Marshy ground
Horsetails	*Equisetum flaviatile*	Marshy ground
	E. arvense	Light soils

reproductive cycle is rather different (see Figure 3.2). Fungi can be very attractive but this usually only applies to their rather transitory fruiting bodies: few are deliberately included in gardens, however. Some mosses may occur and, in damp places, liverworts, but they usually attract little attention.

Figure 3.2 Reproduction in the male fern

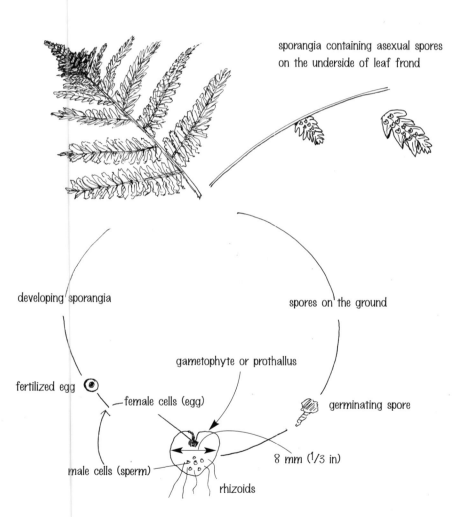

sporangia containing asexual spores on the underside of leaf frond

developing sporangia

spores on the ground

gametophyte or prothallus

fertilized egg

female cells (egg)

germinating spore

8 mm (1/3 in)

male cells (sperm)

rhizoids

Plants of wet places

Bog plants clearly do not worry about waterlogging and their roots either have to obtain oxygen from the water or it is obtained through the above-ground parts. They are often deep-rooted, however, presumably to gain access to nutrients, since these tend to be in rather dilute solution in the water. They include plants such as the iris or yellow flag, which appear to be almost equally at home continually in water or on soil that periodically dries out completely, but also plants such as the bulrush that really only thrive with their roots in water. Bog plants provide good illustrations of the interesting variety of stem shapes and structures that exist (see Box 3.8).

Box 3.8 Stem shape and structure

Some groups of plants can be readily distinguished by the cross-section of their stems, for example

Square-sectioned stems
Labiatae
  Ground ivy
  Catmint
  Dead nettle

Round stems
  Grasses (hollow)
  Rushes (pith-filled)
  Crucifers

Triangular-sectioned stems
  Sedges

Aquatic plants

Truly aquatic plants live only in water, of course, but they are not necessarily submerged. Water lilies combine substantial root systems that often flourish at a depth of 1 m (3¼ ft) or more, with stems that adjust to the depth of water (and can do so in a matter of days), large leaves that spread out (mainly without overlapping) when they reach the surface, and magnificent flowers. These do not usually last very long but keep on coming over a long season. Perhaps because they are not so readily accessible, these are usually allowed to set seed. Since they are never short of water, aquatic plants may grow at enormous rates. The most spectacular are not really desirable in a pond: two common examples are blanket weed (a blue-green alga) and duck weed (*Lemna minor*). Blanket weed can clog up an entire pond in days and be quite difficult to remove, because, although it appears to be a huge green mass, in fact it has little substance and can regenerate from the smallest piece of filament. The high growth rate is due to the exponential increase (see Box 3.9) shown by such simple plants. The danger of dismissing such plants as a menace is illustrated by the excellent protection they afford to newts, newt eggs and larvae, dragonfly nymphs and a host of other insects.

Box 3.9 Exponential growth

Growth can increase in a simple linear fashion but it can also occur by doubling and this is one example of exponential growth, where the rate of growth continually increases. Duckweed (*Lemna* spp.) on a pond or a water butt is a readily observable example.

The plant has a very simple structure (see below) of a small (2-3 mm/^{1}/16 in) flat frond (really a stem) floating on the surface with some fine roots hanging down in the water. It grows by division into two, so one becomes two, two becomes four and so on.

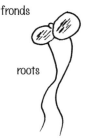

fronds

roots

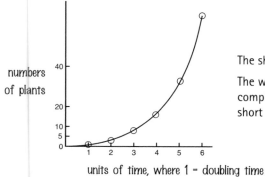

numbers of plants

units of time, where 1 = doubling time

The shape of the growth curve.

The water surface can be completely covered in a very short time.

It seems that a bag of rotting straw – preferably barley – has the effect of greatly reducing the growth rate of blanket weed. Very little straw is required – for example 10 g per 1 m^3 ($\frac{1}{4}$ oz per 1 $\frac{1}{4}$ cu yd) of water – but it takes at least a month to work. I have not always found this to be effective, however.

Duckweed shows exponential growth very clearly because it floats on the surface and you can actually count the number of plants. Such growth is self-limiting, but only when all the available space is filled: it is therefore very difficult to control. However, moorhens – of all ages – are very effective, eating it at a tremendous rate.

Floating plants can engage in the same gaseous exchange (of oxygen and CO_2) as non-aquatic plants: submerged plants derive their CO_2 from the water and give off bubbles of oxygen (visible at higher temperatures) that help to oxygenate the water and thus make it able to support more aquatic animals (including fish). Many of these animals (water beetles, mosquito larvae, water boatmen) come to the surface to breathe, often trapping a bubble of air under their wing cases or in hairs on the surface of the body, but many others are entirely dependent on oxygen dissolved in the water. Aquatic plants are therefore extremely important to aquatic animals, not only for oxygen but also as food, cover for protection, sites for egg-laying and so on. Water without animals is not only less interesting but may be much less attractive. For example, tiny animals eat the tiny plants that can turn the water to a cloudy, impenetrable green.

Just as for terrestrial plants, those that live in water may be annuals, springing up each year from seed that falls into the mud at the bottom of the pond, or perennials (such as the water lily).

Lawns

The essence of lawn grasses is that, because their growing points are close to the ground, they can be cut (or grazed, for that matter), repeatedly without any danger of killing them off. Indeed, they react by branching (called tillering in grasses) and forming an even denser mat. (Hence the advice that to obtain a lawn like that of an Oxford college you only have to cut it frequently – daily at the peak of growth – for about 100 years!) Fine-leaved grasses are usually preferred but, in fact, some of the agricultural grasses such as perennial ryegrass (*Lolium perenne*) will form excellent lawns if cut frequently.

The only time most grasses are damaged by cutting is after they have been allowed to grow tall and set seed. This results in a lot of bare soil between the plants and if this treatment is prolonged, tuft-forming grasses tend to develop – good for voles and ants' nests but not for lawns. On the other hand, many grasses are very decorative when they are flowering and seeding, with species coming into head throughout the spring and summer (see Table 3.4).

Table 3.4 The flowering of grasses

(varies with temperature)

Species	Season of ear initiation	Ear emergence
Ryegrass (*Lolium perenne*)	early to mid-spring	late spring to early summer
Cocksfoot (*Dactylis glomerata*)	mid-spring	late spring
Fescues (*Festuca* spp.)	late winter	mid- to late spring
Timothy (*Phleum pratense*)	mid- to late spring	early summer
Meadow foxtail (*Alopecurus pratensis*)	early to mid-spring	mid- to late spring

Many animals disturb the appearance of a lawn. Some dig holes in it (rabbits, foxes and green woodpeckers), some burrow beneath it (see Chapter 5) and may raise mounds (for example ants and moles), others burrow and leave casts but contribute to drainage and aeration, and others live harmlessly among the grasses, including vast numbers of spiders. The web-forming ones can be seen most easily in autumn, when the presence of dew makes them easily visible.

Gardeners vary greatly in their tolerance for non-grass plants in their lawns. Dandelions are probably universally disliked, daisies somewhat less so, while other small wild flowers and moss give rise to very varied reactions.

Cutting the lawn, depending on the equipment available, is usually regarded as a chore and the possibility of lawns that do not need cutting is attractive. Chamomile (*Anthemis nobilis* or *Matricaria chamomilla*) has been used as an alternative, for example, but it is worth noting that lawnmowing usually removes the cut grass (giving rise to a need to replace nutrients) and thus cleans the lawn at the same time. Lawns do get soiled, for example, with bird droppings, and if grass is not cut and the weather is dry it can get quite contaminated. Whatever we do, the lawn, like the rest of the garden, will harbour a great many harmless (as well as harmful) creatures, all of which are more or less fascinating and attractive and can add to the interest of a garden. These are considered in Chapter 4.

Plants are, of course, cold-blooded (like insects) but that does not mean that they cannot produce heat. This is well known in the case of rotting vegetation (as in composts and, very rapidly, in a heap of lawn-clippings, due to bacterial activity) but is astonishingly true of some living plants. For example, it has recently been shown that aroid plants, including *Philodendron selloum* and *Arum maculatum* (lords and ladies) can raise their temperature (at least in some tissues) to 38°C (100°F) when the ambient temperature is 4°C (39°F) and to 46°C (115°F) when the ambient temperature is 39°C (102°F)! Heat production rates (in watts per gram) have been measured for *Philodendron selloum* at 0.16 to 0.4, compared with 0.016 for a 125 g (5 oz) rat at 10°C and 2.4 for bee flight muscles.

Plants appear to have more senses than are generally recognized. They can smell, taste, touch and perhaps even hear! It has recently been found that the growth rate of dwarf pea plants was increased by sound frequencies at about 2 kilohertz (similar to that of a human voice) but a bit louder (70-80 decibels).

This will be welcome news for those who talk to their plants, but current evidence is that you would have to keep it up for quite a while.

Hedges and trees

Many garden trees attract the same range of insects as other plants but this is even more the case with hedges. They can also act as effective boundaries, especially thorny bushes such as hawthorn, blackthorn, spindle, field maple, hazel and guelder rose. They combine dog- and child-proof fences as well as providing an abundance of nesting sites. Small passerine birds (and those that would prey upon them) depend on hedges to a great extent.

The role of garden plants

Obviously garden plants have many roles related to giving pleasure to the gardener (plus relatives, friends and visitors). To do this in the round, gardeners arrange plants in attractive patterns and functional successions.

But, in addition, it is clear that plants form the basis of all life in the garden; all the animals either feed on them or feed on those that do. So the natural history of a garden is actually determined by the plants that grow there and thus by the gardener.

4 Garden Animals

Gardens are full of animals but they are not usually planned that way. Indeed, most of the animals are very small and well hidden. Apart from birds, larger animals tend to be nocturnal and their numbers are very dependent on the size of the garden. Some, including many birds, are visitors from outside the garden (see Chapter 10): others inhabit the soil (see Chapter 5) and are not normally visible. Water (ponds, lakes, streams) has its own populations of animals (see Chapter 9), but many use the water only for breeding and spend most of the year out of it.

It is, of course, possible to construct a garden that encourages animals, as is often done in planting deliberately to attract butterflies or a range of bee species. The latter add great interest and variety, and are even visually attractive, without any detriment to the plants. This cannot be said for many of the invertebrates which live on the plants and damage them to some extent, reducing their vigour and spoiling their appearance. However, some do no harm (some pollen beetles – there is no shortage of pollen) and others are beneficial, in controlling pests by predation or parasitism. Some, such as the common wasp, are a mixed blessing: they feed their grubs on insects they catch but they may damage fruit and make themselves a nuisance, to put it mildly. However, we cannot choose to have just the beneficial creatures and it is hard to imagine a garden totally without animals; it would not function very well, especially in the soil. A garden without invertebrate animals, for example, would have very few birds.

On the other hand, while we can control what plants are present, the emphasis on animals is usually to ensure that the most pestiferous or obnoxious are absent. Animals cannot be controlled in the same way that plants can: they will not necessarily stay where they are put.

Methods of locomotion

Animals use every conceivable means of locomotion. The most readily observed in the garden are:

Flying Birds, bees, butterflies.

Swimming Frogs, diving beetles, fish, water shrews.

Jumping Grasshoppers, frogs.

Crawling Slugs, snails, toads, caterpillars, centipedes.

Slithering Grass snakes.

Running Mice, beetles, voles, foxes, rabbits.

Walking Stag beetles, greenflies.

Skating Pond skaters, whirligig beetles.

It is worth considering why they move about. Among the most important reasons are: (i) to find food; (ii) to avoid being eaten; (iii) to find a mate; (iv) to find a suitable place to reproduce.

Finding food

No great speed is normally required to find plant food, but that does not rule out the need for mobility. The collection of nectar or pollen, for example, would be very energy-inefficient if an insect had to climb up and down individual plants, so it is generally done by flying insects. When non-flying insects crawl up and down plants, it is often the case that they are predators on creatures that are found in groups or benefit from them: this is well exemplified by ants 'herding' and 'milking' aphids (see Figure 7.1). Ladybirds also feed on aphids and can fly but that is partly in order to lay eggs in another place. Ladybird larvae cannot fly and remain among the aphids, which themselves reproduce quite rapidly.

Animals that live on foliage move from plant to plant, especially if they are relatively large (for example rabbits, deer and voles), are able to fly (for example leaf beetles), are close to the ground (for example slugs and snails), live on the same type of plant more or less continuously (for example caterpillars), or visit plants at night.

Most plant-eating insects lay their eggs on or near the food plant on which their larvae will feed. This is determined by the lack of mobility of the larvae. Examples include the nectar-feeding butterflies and moths. The peacock caterpillars occur only on nettles (see Box 10.6).

In the case of the young of most birds, food is brought to the nest: where this is not so (for example pheasants, partridges, moorhens, ducks), the offspring are mobile almost immediately after hatching. Food plants are identified by smell, taste, touch or appearance, including colour. It now seems that many birds identify berries by reflected ultra-violet light, only shown when the berries are ripe.

Carnivorous animals other than birds may also place their offspring in the region of a source of prey: centipedes reproduce under logs where their prey also hide, ladybirds lay their eggs near greenfly, dragonflies lay their eggs in water where their larvae find the other insects they eat.

Carnivorous mammals (for example foxes, shrews, moles) feed their young – usually in a nest or den – initially on milk and may then bring food to them. Once they become adult, carnivorous animals tend to be very active, since they have to hunt over relatively large areas to find enough food. Thus, owls, foxes and insectivorous birds need territories to ensure adequate feed supplies and this leads to all kinds of behavioural patterns (including much birdsong) designed to establish and hold a territory. Territorial singing in birds is mostly done by the male, as it is for attracting a mate, although female robins regularly sing in winter. Interestingly, birdsong occurs in a frequency range best adapted for efficient transmission through leafy undergrowth.

Without territories, carnivorous animals would be inefficiently searching very large areas in competition with others of the same species. In these ways, then, moving about to collect food is actually organized, and largely vegetarian animals, such as squirrels, may behave in similar ways.

Avoiding being eaten

There are various strategies to avoid being eaten, only some of which depend upon movement.

Butterflies are often quite difficult for birds to catch, not because of their speed but because of their manoeuvrability. Hares and rabbits combine speed and manoeuvrability to dodge foxes and birds of prey. Dragonflies are so fast that they can seize other flying insects on the wing and must themselves be very difficult to catch, except just after they have emerged from their pupal cases.

However, probably most prey try to escape detection by hiding (under stones, vegetation, in crevices or holes in the ground), camouflage (for example stick insects, some caterpillars), warning coloration (for example wasps, see Figure 4.1), by making very little sound, by very unobtrusive movement and, indeed, by remaining quite still for long periods of time.

Although some animals depend almost entirely on camouflage, most blend amazingly well into their chosen backgrounds when they stop moving about. It follows that to see the animals that are actually present in a garden, it is necessary to look closely and carefully at the surfaces they resemble and in the places that they hide, and to be very aware of even slight movement. It is quite astonishing how even quite colourful birds and quite large rabbits blend into the background when they are motionless.

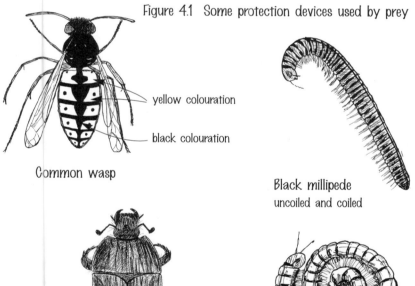

Figure 4.1 Some protection devices used by prey

yellow colouration

black colouration

Common wasp

Black millipede
uncoiled and coiled

Dung beetle

Table 4.1 Protection in invertebrates

Dung beetle (*Geotrupes stercorarius*)	Large blue-black beetle, well protected by armour, often carries little brown mites.
Wood lice (*Isopoda*) (e.g. *Porcellio scaber*)	Hard segmented carapace (a small white species, *Pletyarthrus hoffmanseggi*, lives within ants' nests using repellent glands to put off the ants).
Pill bugs (see Box 11.1) (*Diplopoda*) (e.g. *Armadillidium vulgare*)	Hard carapace segmented to roll into a ball or coil.
and millipedes (e.g. *Cylindroiulus londinensis*)	Hard segmented exoskeleton, with 2 pairs of legs per segment: coils up when disturbed.
Stag beetle (*Lucanus cervus*)	Powerful jaws and armoured body (as with many beetles – and there are c. 4000 species in Britain).

Hiding is often a way of life and earwigs and centipedes automatically creep into crevices until both surfaces of their flattened bodies touch the sides. Froghoppers stay within the 'cuckoo-spit' froth they produce and woodlice, pill bugs and shield bugs are well protected by a horny covering (see Table 4.1).

Finding a mate
This rarely depends upon sight alone and frequently sight is a barely a significant factor. After all, the ways in which animals avoid detection also apply to those seeking a mate. So, at the appropriate times, animals give signals that alert the opposite sex of the same species, generally at a distance too great to be useful to a predator.

Female moths, for example, give off a scent, or pheromone, at concentrations undetectable by most other animals but enough for the male of the same species to detect over a distance of several miles (see Box 4.1). This is one reason why so many moths have large, feathery antennae: butterflies by contrast have antennae that end in club-like structures (see Figure 4.2) which are not found in moths.

Box 4.1 Pheromones

Plants and animals release biologically active compounds called semio-chemicals that affect others, often at a considerable distance. The best known are the 'pheromones' released by female moths that attract males from up to 8 km (5 miles) away. (Hormones, conversely, are internal signals which mainly affect the organism producing them.) The moth's sensors can respond to a single molecule of a pheromone. Male bumble-bees use pheromones (from their mouths) to mark mating perches where females will await their return.

When some plants are attacked by insects (for example caterpillars on maize or corn), they give off a blend of volatile terpenoids (which give the characteristic smell to pine resin) that attract parasitic wasps to home in on the caterpillars. This has now been found to be not uncommon and, amazingly, that the message can alert undamaged plants and result in their protection.

Aphids produce 'alarm' pheromones (also terpenoids) that cause other aphids to spread out, thus making them more difficult to harvest by predators – but easier for the gardener to reach with chemicals.

Why is this? Antennae are organs of smell and touch and perhaps moths, which are largely nocturnal, need a greater sense of smell, to find food and mates: butterflies may rely more on sight.

Figure 4.2 Typical antennae of moth (left) and butterfly

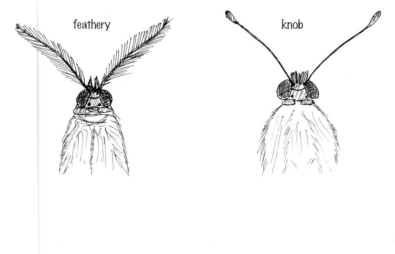

feathery   knob

Comparable methods of communication must operate in water (presumably by 'taste') since many aquatic animals (for example newts) seem to have rather limited vision and, in any case, the water may be cloudy or the animals may frequently be hiding in the mud. Insects that live in water as larvae, often synchronize their emergence as adults (for example the mayfly) to improve their chance of meeting a mate.

Other animals detect each other by vibration and, in soil and within timber, this may occur as noise. Animals that dwell on the surface of the water (for example pond-skaters) detect their prey by vibrations and then move towards them. Web-making spiders remain stationary until their prey vibrates the web and male spiders, often consumed by the larger females after (or even before) mating, have to approach with great caution, giving out recognizable vibrations as they advance.

Animals that live in colonies have less of a problem finding a mate. Ants swarm (in their winged phase) in order to increase the chances of males and females encountering one another.

Birds are well equipped to find mates, being able to fly rapidly in response to even distant signals, commonly song but, in greater and lesser spotted woodpeckers, for example, rapid drumming against tree branches. The lesser spotted produces a much higher tone and, in both species, this is quite different from the noises made in searching for insects or drilling a nest hole. Birds also have characteristic colours which serve for recognition and commonly for display.

Many mammals deliberately scent-mark their boundaries, either to establish territories or to signal to prospective partners. They also use sound, well illustrated by the characteristic barking of foxes.

Finding a place to reproduce

This requires a great deal of searching in order to find a site that is likely to be both suitable and secure. Birds are the most noticeable in this activity, although it is often quite difficult to find their nests because of their extreme caution in visiting them. Even when nest-building or feeding young, when their beaks are clearly full of nesting material or food, they will move indirectly to their nests or wait until they are satisfied that they are not being observed – by humans, squirrels, jays or magpies, in particular.

However, long before this, many species of birds can be observed exploring potential sites, even as early as late autumn. This is particularly noticeable with birds that nest in existing holes, for example tits, stock doves and nuthatches, although starlings seem only to become interested nearer to nesting time.

In the case of birds, gardeners commonly put up nest boxes and these are well used, in spite of being readily observed – perhaps they are constructed and sited so that access is difficult for their enemies, and this may give birds the confidence to lessen their extreme caution. This may be the reason why house-martins will build their nests in full view of humans and come and go readily, even returning to the same nests each year. Blue and great tits are the most common occupants of nest boxes; owls and bats may be provided with platforms or refuges and this may make possible the presence of breeding pairs or colonies where otherwise no suitable sites exist.

Some insects can also be provided with breeding sites, notably bumble-bees, just as hives are provided for honey-bees, but those whose larvae feed on plants will only reproduce where the appropriate species occur. Bumble-bees can be enticed to nest in moss-filled pots or boxes with a mousehole-sized entrance: in fact, they appear to be attracted by the smell of mice or voles and often use their tunnels.

Solitary bees, such as the red mason bee (*Osmia rufa*) can be attracted to nest in cardboard or plastic tubes, like large straws. These can be packed together and placed in a sunny, south-facing position. These bees do not usually sting, do not swarm, do not suffer from varroa and are said to be much more active pollinators than honey-bees.

Many small invertebrates, including slugs and snails, use crevices to withdraw to and to lay their eggs in: others reproduce in the soil, either in cracks or tunnels that they excavate (for example mining bees and digger wasps).

Mammals are in many ways the least noticeable, even when they are quite big. Deer may be rarely seen even though they may visit gardens (mainly at night), badgers are notoriously difficult to observe, even though their setts may be obvious, and the smaller mammals, such as mice and voles, may not be seen at all unless special measures are adopted (see Chapter 11).

If the garden contains a pond (see Chapter 9), many fascinating invertebrates will breed in it (including pond snails, beetles, pond-skaters, water-boatmen, mayflies, caddis flies and dragonflies), as will vertebrates such as frogs, toads and newts, all of which are beneficial but will only visit the water during the breeding season. It is often said that frogs and newts return to the same pond (or the one they were reared in) but it is also true that completely new ponds are colonized very quickly. Certainly, there are cases of newts and toads breeding in ponds less than a year after their construction, as long as they provide suitable conditions (plants, accessible edges, preferred depth, food sources and so on), even in areas where no shortage of other ponds exists.

Very often, it is only at these seasons of reproductive activity that some animals (such as newts) are seen at all, and frog-spawn may be the most obvious sign that frogs are present. This raises the question of actually observing animals in the garden.

Observing animals

Partly because they move about, hide away and are often nocturnal or crepuscular, many species are not seen at all – or very rarely. However, to a large extent we see what we are looking for and that depends upon knowing that it may be there and what signs can be used as indicators of its presence.

Many insects and other small invertebrates can be discovered if their hiding places are inspected but even larger animals are very skilled at avoiding observation, since otherwise they or their offspring would get eaten. This is so for many common birds but quite often their behaviour can be interpreted: even so, it is extremely hard to discover where most garden birds spend the night. Of course, nocturnal animals (bats, many amphibians, moths, owls, foxes, badgers, mice) are generally only seen after dark.

There are thus two opposing strategies for observing animals: active, scouting, and sitting still. Few gardeners seem inclined to do the latter, and so will rarely see more nervous animals.

Animal behaviour

Before discussing our view of how animals behave, it is worth acknowledging the extent to which they interpret our behaviour. It has long been held that wood-pigeons react quite differently to humans if they observe they are carrying guns and most of us have experienced the greater confidence that many birds show when it is obvious that we are working. This may be partly due to the fact that we remain, obviously harmless, in the same area of garden or woodland, and it helps, of course, if our actions (for example digging) are exposing food. Robins in particular will practically join in and perch on tools and wheelbarrows, the better to detect and exploit the food supply, but other birds and some mammals, especially grey squirrels, quite quickly adjust to what they perceive as a harmless presence. However, behaviour such as carrying food or nesting material generally makes most birds more cautious.

People, on the other hand, tend to be slow to interpret animal behaviour, partly because it does not occur to them that it is possible and partly due to fear of being anthropomorphic (while having no such inhibition about their pets). Yet we all interpret the behaviour of other people: 'He was behaving very suspiciously,' we say, or 'She was overjoyed/sad/annoyed/unmoved.' We are particularly reluctant to attribute emotions to animals, especially birds – perhaps because the structure of their 'faces' virtually precludes the expression of them. However, it is surprising how often it is worth asking, 'What is it up to?' when observing an animal.

It is often quite clear when a bird is collecting food for itself or for its offspring, collecting nesting material (in some cases, like crows, breaking off pliant twigs and shoots), or enticing you away from its nest or defending territory. It is less obvious when birds, even as early as late autumn, are prospecting for nest sites for the following spring: indeed, it is really only clear in the case of hole-nesting birds.

Squirrels' behaviour is easy to spot when they are burying acorns, but on occasion they appear just to be having fun, or practising their acrobatic skills. Frogs and toads are at their least acrobatic at mating time and their clumsy splashing about is very noticeable because they are coupled, the male clasping its forearms round the female until spawning is complete. The reason is that the eggs swell up in water

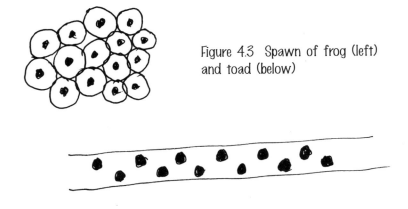

Figure 4.3 Spawn of frog (left) and toad (below)

very quickly to form the well-known masses of jelly-like frog-spawn and double chains of toad-spawn (see Figure 4.3) and, in order that they can be fertilized, the male has to release the sperm more or less simultaneously over the newly laid eggs as otherwise the sperm cannot penetrate the jelly.

Very often, animal behaviour is purposive and the purpose can be deduced. For example, you can see whether bees are collecting nectar or pollen and it is often easy to see that a queen bumble-bee is searching for a new nest site, though it is rare to observe a firm decision. Sometimes, it is even possible to deduce that it has not yet found one from the fact that its upper thorax is covered in mites (see Box 7.8), since they drop off in the new nest.

Digger wasps (see Box 2.4) can be seen excavating their holes in the ground and stocking them with paralysed prey (spiders, flies, small bees), and in spite of the care they take to orient themselves it is astonishing how often they make mistakes and enter the wrong burrow. Where such wasps have 'colonies' of burrows, it is also easy to observe parasitic wasps, especially the colourful ruby-tailed wasp (*Chrysis cyanea* and other species) waiting to take advantage of an absentee in order to nip in and lay an egg on that of the digger wasp. Such parasites seem to have no difficulty in telling whether a burrow is occupied or not, but then, it is astounding how they find the burrows in the first place.

Animal signs

It is, of course, only those animals that are readily seen where it is possible to study their behaviour and try to interpret it. For those that are not easy to see, observation has to focus on signs.

Sounds

The barking of foxes, the croaking of frogs, the buzzing of bees and the drumming of woodpeckers are signs of often unseen presences.

Tracks

Tracks sometimes provide evidence, especially in snow, of foxes, badgers and birds but this only applies to a rather small number of species. Snail and slug tracks can be seen wherever they have travelled over their own slimy excretion.

Excreta

Excreta offer strong clues, sometimes that animals have passed that way but sometimes of residence (see Table 4.2). So much of a give-away would bird droppings be below nest sites that the adults regularly remove the droppings of nestlings (produced in the form of whitish bags) and deposit them at a considerable distance from the nest. This also keeps the nest uncontaminated, though not all birds do this and nests can become filthy and infested with invertebrates, some of them parasitic.

The activity of bats can be deduced from the number of droppings (like small black grains of rice) below their roosts.

Barn owl pellets are ejected and contain inedible remnants of their meals, such as fur and bones. You can therefore tell what they have been eating, as you can with fox excreta.

Plant damage

Tunnels in leaves show up clearly (see page 51), as do areas that have been eaten. Many tunnels show up as light-coloured, wandering lines. They are caused by leaf-miners burrowing between the leaf surfaces. Caterpillars of a moth (*Nepticula aurella*) do this in blackberry leaves. Quite often leaves are rolled up in response to damage by insects, while other creatures (for example many

Table 4.2 Clues from excreta

Droppings from	Appearance	Site
Bats	Small near-black elongated pellets (c. 3 mm/^{1}/16 in long)	Under roosts, in roof spaces, etc.
Rabbits	Fibrous grey-brown pellets	Mainly concentrated at special points in their territory
Voles	Small olive-coloured elongated pellets	Concentrated in separate nest hollows among their tunnels in long grass
Foxes	Smaller and darker version of dog faeces, often full of hair and fur, especially at the (often) curled end	Anywhere
Shrews	Larger and darker than those of voles, moist, cylindrical	At or near nest sites
Birds	Varies with the bird – some (e.g. heron) identifiable from large size	Mainly seen under roosting sites

caterpillars) fasten the sides of leaves together with silk to form a protective sheath. Most common leaf-rollers are moth caterpillars. Spiders, which feed mainly on insects not plants, also do this to form a brood chamber and may be found guarding their eggs or young.

Leaves and shoots grazed off by rabbits or deer are only too obvious and rabbits will also dig small holes in the surface of a lawn, sometimes in a line which they seem to play along. The semicircular cuts, notably in rose leaves (but also lilac, laburnum, willow), made by leaf-cutter bees are usually neither serious nor disfiguring: they are carted off by solitary bees (*Megachile* spp.) to line their tunnels, forming tubular cells in which eggs are laid on provisions of pollen. These bees actually cut different shapes for different parts of the tube, especially the ends, and this makes one wonder whether instinct is enough for this or whether intelligence is also needed.

Deformations of plant growth (for example galls) are also evidence of pests or disease and thus often reveal the presence of small animals. The number and variety are astonishing – 56 different types of gall have been found on a single English oak tree, for example.

Barking of trees may be done by squirrels or rabbits and can be very damaging, but it may also occur on the shoots that willows quite naturally shed, if other food is in short supply (at the end of a hard winter or during a late spring).

Food remains
Sometimes parts of carcasses betray the activities of a carnivore. Even feathers can tell us something. For example, the quills are cut cleanly by foxes but chewed by mustelids (for example stoats and weasels).

Disturbed earth
Molehills are the obvious example and there is a theory that there is no need to destroy the moles, only to remove the molehills (the mole's way of disposing of the results of tunnelling). The idea is that the mole will continue to use the tunnels, collecting mainly earthworms, without producing more hills. However, many moles are clearly not familiar with this theory and continually move on to fresh fields and pastures new, marking their progress in the usual way.

Earthworm casts displease many gardeners but are dispersed, of course, during lawnmowing. Only two species of earthworm produce these casts, *Allolobophora longa* and *A. nocturna*, and even these rest in a dry summer (called the summer diapause).

Some burrows, such as those of the rabbit, can hardly be missed but others would escape detection by most people. These are made by solitary bees (for example *Andrena* spp.) and solitary wasps (for example *Cerceris* spp.) and, although marked by small conical mounds of soil particles, are quite hard to see in a lawn. Even when they occur, as they often do, on bare earthen paths or between bricks on a path or patio, they frequently escape notice.

Wood excavations
Wood-boring beetles (such as the powder post beetles, *Lyctus* spp.) produce a fine dust – often the first alarming sign of damage to

structures but commonly from tiny holes bored in old posts or other dead wood.

The most spectacular examples in the excavation category are the wood chippings produced by woodpeckers (see Box 4.2). I am fortunate that all three British species of woodpecker (see Box 4.2) breed in my garden: they all drill holes, generally new ones each year. Although you may hear the birds chipping out their holes (quite different from their drumming), they are extremely difficult to locate and the easiest way to detect them is to observe the chips of wood below. They land on the soil but also on vegetation and, by brushing it off the plants and observing when new chips arrive, you can follow the progress of excavations even when you cannot see the hole itself.

Box 4.2 Woodpeckers

There are three British species, not uncommon in large gardens but rarer in the north. They are: green woodpecker *Picus viridus* (jackdaw-sized); great spotted woodpecker *Dendrocopus major* (thrush-sized); and lesser spotted woodpecker *Dendrocopus minor* (sparrow-sized). All three nest in holes in trees, which they rarely re-use: the size of the nest-hole is related to the size of the bird, so it is clear whose it is. The holes may be drilled any time from late autumn onwards but nesting is usually in mid-spring.

The spotted woodpeckers both 'drum' rapidly, usually high up on dead wood; this can be heard for a long way but is difficult to observe. The green woodpecker does not drum but has a strange 'laughing' call (giving rise to the country name 'yaffle'). The drumming is very rapid (for example 18 beats per second) and is possible because woodpeckers have a cartilage 'shock-absorber' at the base of the bill and their tongues, which are up to 5 cm (2 in) long, actually surround the brain when not extended. A lesser spotted woodpecker has been timed at 33 hits in 1.13 seconds!

These woodpeckers are all insectivorous, mostly collecting from the bark of trees or from dead wood, but the green woodpecker is often seen on lawns licking up ants (which it can regurgitate to feed the young). It has a curious crouching posture (because of the short legs that are characteristic of birds that creep up trees) with its beak often pointing up at an angle of about 45 degrees. Spotted woodpeckers also eat nuts and feed their young on tortrix caterpillars on oak trees – as do blue tits.

Shed skins

Many animals shed their skins at intervals and their (past) presence may be indicated by these cast-offs. The most noticeable are snake skins which can be quite large and include the skin over the head and eyes, and the pupal cases of dragonflies, left on rushes, for example, at the edge of ponds.

Reproduction

The search for food and the reproduction of the species are two fundamentals of animal behaviour. Animals reproduce in a variety of ways, varying greatly between species and, in some important ways, between orders.

Mammals

Mammals, by definition, produce milk and feed their young on it from birth to weaning, though the latter takes place at widely differing ages. The size of the litter varies, as does the number of litters per year. These variations are illustrated for garden mammals in Table 4.3. Mammals are the only animals with mammary glands but many others secrete substances for their young to feed on (for example pigeon's 'milk', from the crop).

Some young are born helpless – blind, hairless and largely immobile (for example rabbits): others are born fully formed and ready to move off within a few hours (for example hares). It follows that the degree of parental care varies greatly and takes different forms.

Birds

It is well known that all birds lay eggs (of variable shape, size, colour, number) in one or more clutches, mostly in their own nests (cuckoos being the exception), in a variety of sites (on the ground, floating on water, high in trees, low in hedges, in holes). The nests vary from huge constructions (for example herons, crows), sometimes with a roof (for example magpies), to delicately constructed and lined structures (for example wrens, finches, hedge sparrows). Some holes are lined and some nests are mere platforms of a few twigs (for

Table 4.3 Litter size in garden mammals

	Typical no. of offspring in one litter	No. of litters per year
Deer	usually 1	1
Badger	2	1
Fox	5	1
Rabbit	3–5	2
Squirrel	3–4	1–2
Weasel	4–6	2
Rat	7–8	5
Field mouse	2–9	6
House mouse	3–5	10
Vole	5	3–6
Hedgehog	3–7	2
Shrew	6–7	2
Mole	3–4	1
Bat (pipistrelle)	1	1

example wood-pigeons). Some nests are built of mud (for example house martins) glued together by saliva, others are lined with mud (for example song thrush and some blackbirds).

It follows that some species can be identified by their nests and most by their eggs, the size of which appears to be remarkably constant for the species. The diameter of every stock dove egg I have measured has been almost exactly 29 mm ($1^{1}/_{8}$ in)!

The task of building the nest (see Box 4.3) and, indeed, incubating the eggs and feeding the young is sometimes the responsibility of one sex only and sometimes shared. Eggs hatch over varying periods (see Table 4.4) and the young require varying degrees of parental care (see Boxes 4.4. and 4.5).

Box 4.3 Nest building

Birds build many different kinds of nests in a wide variety of sites. Few are easily seen and it is usually difficult to observe them being built. However, birds carrying nesting material are quite easy to spot and close observation can often tell you what stage the nest construction has reached. For example, song thrushes line their nests with a smooth layer of mud. They can be seen collecting it and this indicates the final stages. Blackbirds, on the other hand, line their nests with mud but at the penultimate stage, and a final lining (of dried grass, for example) is added while the mud is still moist: it therefore gets embedded in it. The diameter of the nest cup is about the same for both song thrushes and blackbirds – 85 mm ($3^3/8$ in). House martins are easily observed both collecting mud and adding it to the nest cup.

A less easily observed mud-user is the nuthatch. Both sexes of this pretty little bird help in collecting mud which they use to reduce the size of the entrance to the woodpecker hole they have chosen to nest in. They choose those made by green or great spotted woodpeckers, whose nests may be capacious (for example 150–230 mm/6–9 in deep), but whose entrance holes are much bigger than the nuthatches need.

Species	Approximate dimensions of entrance hole	
Green woodpecker	80 x 70 mm	($3^1/8$ x $2^3/4$ in)
Great spotted woodpecker	70 x 75 mm	($2^3/4$ x 3 in)
Lesser spotted woodpecker	44 x 50 mm	($1^3/4$ x 2 in)
Nuthatch	25 x 30 mm	(1 x $1^1/4$ in)

Wrens' nests are sometimes very obvious, when built among roof timbers, for example, but they also nest in holes in trees and cracks in brickwork that lead to spaces. The nest is usually completely roofed in and entered by a small hole in the side: the male builds several and offers them for choice by the female.

Robins build very neat nests, often lined with feathers and often constructed mainly of moss. Not all birds line their nests, however. Woodpeckers hollow out very substantial nest holes (often in willows – where the wood is not too hard – or in dead trees beginning to rot) but do not line them at all.

Wood-pigeons are remarkable for the slightness of the platform they build, consisting of a collection of twigs but, precarious though they appear, the nests will often still be there more than a year later. Perhaps there is more to the construction than is immediately apparent to us: in fact, the twigs used are often intertwined so that the nest can be lifted as a whole without falling apart.

Crows, on the other hand, build very substantial nests but, if they are observed closely, the birds (both sexes) can be seen carrying, first, substantial twigs, then pliable twigs broken off living trees (to be woven into the nest, where they dry in position), and finally a lining (of dead leaves, for example). All this can be observed when they nest in deciduous trees because crows generally build their nests before the leaves appear. Crows' nests may remain for more than a year but are not necessarily re-used. Squirrels may build a dray on top. Magpies are the only large birds to construct their nests with substantial roofs.

Few species re-use a nest the following year, probably because of a build-up of parasites and the fact that its position may by then be obvious. House martins are one exception, in spite of the fact that house martins may harbour an unusual number of fleas – several thousand in one nest. However, water birds often use the same sites in successive years. In the case of ducks, little remains of the previous nest and even moorhens' nests, which are often quite elaborate structures, do not survive intact, sometimes due to flooding. Even neat and tidy nests, like those built by robins, may be trampled almost flat by the nestlings before they leave.

Robins may build their nests up against the walls of a house and martins build under the eaves, but jackdaws will actually penetrate inside the house, at least as far as an unused chimney. They drop twigs down and construct a nest where the bigger ones lodge. They can be seen perched on, and diving down, the chimney pot, carrying twigs and, later, food for their young. Wasps will also build in attics and may construct very large nests from chewed-up wood. Within the outer wall, row upon row of neat hexagonal cells are constructed.

Table 4.4 Reproduction in garden birds

	Clutch size	Incubation period (days)
Wood-pigeon	2	17
House martin	4–5	13–19
Blackbird	4–5	11–17
Song thrush	4–6	11–15
Robin	5–6	12–15
Blue tit	7–12	12–16

	Clutch size	Incubation period (days)
Great tit	8–13	13–14
Starling	5–7	12–15
House sparrow	3–5	11–14
Chaffinch	4–5	11–13
Mallard	7–12	28–29
Moorhen	5–11	19–22
Green woodpecker	5–7	18–19

Box 4.4 Parental care

This may take many forms, the most familiar being the nesting of birds and the suckling of mammalian young. The purposes are to take the young from a dependent stage to one of independence, in terms of feeding, ability to regulate temperature, move about, avoid predators, seek shelter and so on.

Where the young are born or hatched in a fully independent form, there may be little or no parental care (as with snakes), but this is also the case for those that go through independent larval stages (caterpillars of butterflies and moths, nymphs of dragonflies). In some cases, as with solitary bees and wasps, the eggs are laid on provisions of food (for example pollen or paralysed prey) and in social insects (honey-bees and common wasps) there is an elaborate social structure, with workers feeding, grooming and protecting the grubs in cells within the hive or nest. There is great variation between species: for example, in some centipedes – but not all – the females will protect their eggs for several weeks, and the young for up to eight weeks after hatching.

Parental care also occurs in some surprising cases: eight are briefly mentioned below.

Sticklebacks
The male fish builds a barrel-like nest, maintains a current of water over the eggs and defends the offspring.

Cyclops
A tiny crustacean (<4 mm/$^1/_8$ in long) commonly found in ponds, the cyclops carries its eggs around with it, in sacs that can easily be seen with the naked eye until they hatch (see Figure 9.5).

Earwigs (*Forficular auricularia*)
Earwigs lay their eggs in a cavity they excavate in the soil and guard their eggs and young until the nymphs can look after themselves. They are thought to lick their eggs in order to prevent mould growth.

Spiders
There are some spiders that lay their eggs in a silken shelter and guard them and the emergent young until they are big enough to fend for themselves. Some of these can be detected because the silk draws the edges of a leaf together (for example on apple trees). For more information about spiders see Box 4.5.

Slugs
Some slugs carry their eggs in a liquid-filled brood pouch for a month.

Shield bugs (*Elasmostethus griseus*)
This species lays up to 30 eggs underneath a birch leaf and remains covering them with the female's body even after they hatch.

Woodlice
The females carry their eggs on the underside of their bodies until they hatch.

Harvestmen
The females carry their eggs in their jaws – and thus cannot feed until they hatch.

Box 4.5 Spiders

Many people dislike spiders but rarely kill them: some suffer from an unreasonable but very real fear (arachniphobia), which can usually be cured but by quite special efforts (and not by saying, 'Don't be silly!'). However, many of those who start off disliking them change their minds completely when they discover how harmless and interesting they are.

Spiders are very numerous (up to 2.5m per 0.4 ha/1 acre of long grass) and the total number for England and Wales has been estimated at 2,200,000,000,000. All are carnivorous and it has been estimated that each spider eats about 100 insects each year, giving a total of 220,000,000,000,000 (weighing more than the human population!). They therefore consume more insects than do birds and are a major part of biological control (see Chapter 8).

Not all spiders spin webs although all of them wrap their eggs in silken cocoons: the zebra spider (see page 22) and the wolf spiders chase after or jump on their prey. Those that do, spin silken webs of various kinds (see Table below), some of which are designed to protect their young.

Common name	Latin name	Nature of web
House spider	*Tegenaria* spp.	Triangular hammocks or cobwebs
Wolf spider	*Pisaura mirabilis*	A tent or wigwam, tying together grass and other leaves, to shelter the cocoon and hatched young
Garden spider	*Theridion sisyphium*	Trellis with conical tent on top containing bluish-green cocoon
	Theridion notatum	Tent with females hanging downwards and feeding the young on regurgitated fluids
	Aranea diadema	Orb web with centre, radial threads and spirals crossing them (about 40 species build orb webs)
Money spider	*Thyreosthenius becki*	Woven gossamer sheets on grass

Parental care occurs in several species. For example, the female wolf spider (*Pisaura mirabilis*), which spins a protective tent, has carried a large cocoon full of eggs around for some time, and when they hatch (in the tent), she remains on guard for several days. In another wolf spider, *Pardosa amentata*, the female also carries a cocoon but, when the eggs hatch, the young ride on her back for a few days. All these are commonly found species that can easily be seen in gardens, and the parental care examples are more readily observed than the adults alone.

Spiders need to be distinguished from the related harvestmen, which are also mainly carnivorous but neither spin nor poison. They are nocturnal and have eight legs but they have undivided, globular bodies, often measuring several centimetres across the legs. Spiders will not eat them and they, like some slugs, carry tiny red mites (also eight-legged arachnoids – reminding one of the 'bigger fleas have smaller fleas' sequence!). Harvestmen may be short-legged (for example *Oligolophus tridens*) or long-legged (for example *Leiobunum rotundum*).

Spiders in the bath

Hardly a garden topic but certainly a household one. 'Why do I find spiders in the bath?' is a commonly asked question. The answer is because they are there and cannot get out. Drape a cloth over the side of the bath and they will soon climb out. At night, when they are about and you are not, they probably fall in by accident.

Snakes

Snakes either lay eggs (for example grass snake) or, like the adder, are viviparous (that is, give birth to live young). Grass snake eggs are rather leathery and take a time to hatch, varying with the temperature: the young then go off on their own. The eggs are laid within a mass of stable manure or fermenting vegetation, which generates heat.

Amphibians

Amphibians (frogs, toads, newts) all lay eggs in water (see Figure 4.4), and all hatch into legless tadpoles (sometimes called newtpoles in the case of newts) which gradually develop limbs and absorb their tails (except in the case of newts), to emerge from the water after several months.

Figure 4.4 Amphibian life cycles

Frog

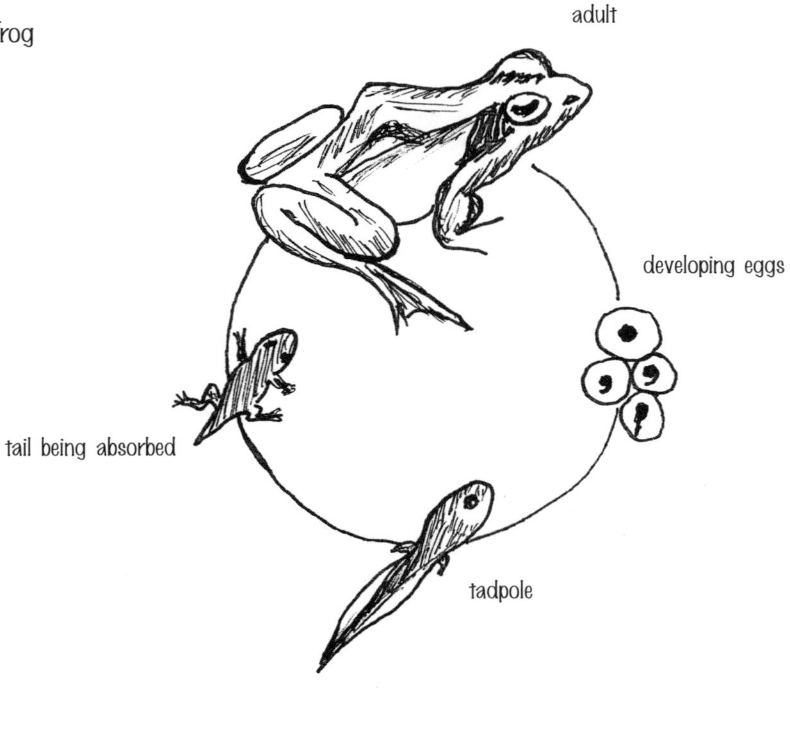

adult

developing eggs

tadpole

tail being absorbed

Newt

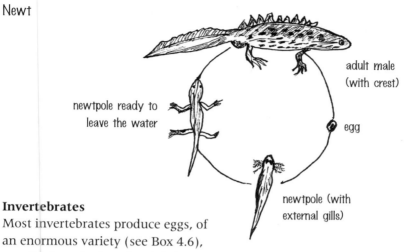

adult male
(with crest)

newtpole ready to
leave the water

egg

newtpole (with
external gills)

Invertebrates

Most invertebrates produce eggs, of
an enormous variety (see Box 4.6),
usually deposited so that (a) they are
hidden or protected from predators (and parasites – but these are
very skilled at finding them), (b) they are protected from the
elements (drying out, freezing, being washed away) and (c) the
emerging young can readily find food. These precautions are needed
because eggs are very vulnerable and immobile, and even the young
are generally much less mobile than the adults. Some eggs, such as
those of snails and slugs can often be found for example under logs,
but some centipedes roll their eggs in soil to disguise them.

Box 4.6 Invertebrate eggs

The variety of eggs found, even within the insects alone, is so great that no
comprehensive description can be attempted. However, there are some very
common examples likely to be encountered by any gardener; some of them are
very beautiful (although this may require a magnifying glass to appreciate), some
are extraordinary and some are plain and not very attractive, but it's nice to know
who they belong to. Here are a few illustrations.

Mosquito eggs
The culex mosquito lays its eggs on any water surface (have a look at your water
butt) in the form of a raft containing up to 300 eggs, which floats and is
remarkably buoyant. When the eggs hatch, the familiar larvae simply wriggle
downwards into the water, where they live by filtering suspended particles of
organic matter out of the water.

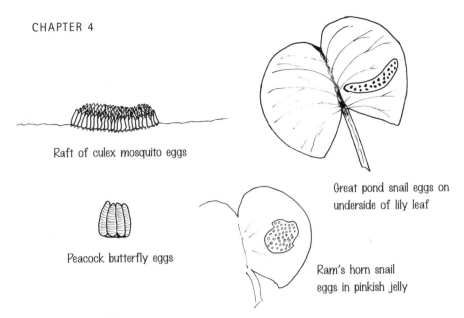

Raft of culex mosquito eggs

Great pond snail eggs on underside of lily leaf

Peacock butterfly eggs

Ram's horn snail eggs in pinkish jelly

Peacock butterfly

The egg is upright, olive-green, with eight prominent ribs from base to a central depression on the top, laid mostly in mid- and late spring on the underside of young leaves of the common stinging nettle.

Lacewing eggs

Lacewing flies are themselves very beautiful (often iridescent blue, green or brown) and often lay eggs on stalks – quite visible to the naked eye. The green lacewings (which eat aphids) produce smooth ovoid eggs, each on the end of a stalk, attached to leaves or on wooden surfaces. This is done by depositing a drop of sticky fluid, drawing it up with the tip of the abdomen to form a rapidly hardening stalk and then laying the egg on the top of it.

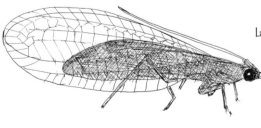

Lacewing fly (60-70 mm/2-3 in long)

Lacewing eggs (on 7 mm/$1/4$ in stalks)

It is an obviously sensible habit, common to many creatures, to lay the eggs on young leaves that are not about to die and drop off.

Snails
Terrestrial snails (such as *Helix aspersa*) and slugs lay spherical creamy-white eggs about 1–2 mm (^{1}/32 in) in diameter in damp earthy places, such as under logs or stones. More spectacular are the eggs laid by the two largest aquatic snails (see opposite). The great pond snail (*Lymnaea stagnalis*) lays gelatinous sausage-shaped strings of eggs (often >25 mm/1 in in length) mainly on the undersides of lily leaves where these are available and, since they are transparent, it is easy to see the whole development of the young. This is also true of the ram's horn snail (*Planorbis corneus*) but the eggs are laid in a flat mass with a slightly pinkish tinge.

Pond snail
wedge-shaped
feelers

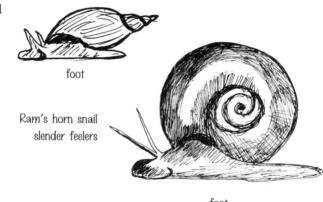

foot

Ram's horn snail
slender feelers

foot

Some invertebrates produce living young, including aphids (in spring and summer), which can easily be observed actually giving birth: this is also an example of parthenogenesis, that is, reproduction without mating. Indeed, in some of the saw-flies and gall wasps, no males are ever found.

In general, animals that form the prey of others reproduce in enormous numbers, relatively few of which survive for very long. Even a successful insect like the ant, which reproduces rapidly and defends its nest, often with specialized 'soldier' ants, can do nothing to avoid the strong beak and long sticky tongue of the green woodpecker.

CHAPTER 4

Growth

Animal young are generally, of necessity, fairly small and a very great increase in size is needed to produce another adult. This is usually accompanied by changes in form and complexity in the relative size of parts, specialization of tissues and a host of other changes. In some animals (for example mice, foxes, spiders), these changes are gradual and continuous. In others (for example butterflies, dragonflies), abrupt changes occur from one state to another and the early stages bear no resemblance to the adult whatever. Sometimes, as in grasshoppers, the form is similar throughout but, because of the rigid exoskeleton, growth has to proceed in stages, with a moult between each one and the next. The young are called nymphs. The example of butterflies and moths is familiar, with caterpillars growing steadily bigger and then pupating, during which time the entire body is reorganized, to emerge in the totally different adult form. These various growth patterns are further discussed in Box 4.7.

Box 4.7 Growth patterns

Those animals that do not start as miniature adults and simply grow bigger (although the proportions change markedly), go through a variety of stages (called 'instars' in insects). The caterpillar of the large white butterfly (*Pieris brassicae*) is a familiar example. The caterpillars (which have a disagreeable smell) feed on the brassicas on which the eggs are laid, usually in groups on the outside of the plant – often quite conspicuous. When they reach their full size, having moulted four times to accommodate growth, they migrate to a sheltered position on a wall, tree, fence or under a window-sill, to pupate. Incidentally, adult numbers are frequently reinforced by large migrations from mainland Europe (as with red admirals). The pupal case or chrysalis of the large white is attached by the tail to the surface but kept upright by a silken girth. The adults emerge in late summer or autumn and overwinter in this condition.

Snails and slugs grow from miniature to full-size versions, which must be quite a problem for a snail, having to increase its shell size gradually and more or less continuously.

Many beetles have grubs quite unlike themselves, which in some cases take years to reach full size (for example stag beetles). It would be impossible to grow steadily from miniature to adult given the very hard and rigid exoskeleton (made of chitin – a very resistant substance, which often appears, especially as wing-cases, in the excreta of beetle-eating birds and mammals).

Nutrition

Of course, growth can only occur if animals are adequately fed and, although the nutrient requirements of most animals are similar (in the sense that they have to supply energy and the substances needed to make proteins and fat), it is quite astonishing what a range of extraordinary diets can supply them.

So, some caterpillars (for example of peacock and red admiral butterflies) live entirely on stinging nettles, yet the butterflies live only on nectar. Voles are largely vegetarian, mice eat grain, insects, nuts and so on, and shrews live on insects, woodlice and snails – yet they all produce furry little warm-blooded bodies, in which the cells, nerves, bones and muscles appear to be remarkably similar.

Most animals need water but many live on very little and obtain all they need in their food. Their ability to live on such diverse diets is largely due to having digestive systems adapted to utilize them. Some animals (aphids, moths) can only use fluids, others can chew their food and discard bits (as with squirrels and mice shelling nuts – see Figure 4.5), while owls, for example, swallow fur, bones and all and eject these unwanted bits in regurgitated pellets. Rabbits produce soft pellets that are eaten again (called 'refection'), thus providing a second passage through the gut for further digestion. The digestive systems of animals are thus very varied (see Figure 4.6) and different parts are designed to perform different functions.

When the food has been digested, nutrients have to be absorbed through the walls of the gut and circulated in the bloodstream to where they are needed (in growing tissues) or stored (fat deposits). Vertebrates have muscular hearts which pump the blood around, but in many invertebrates there is no circulatory system and the body organs are simply bathed in the blood fluid.

In vertebrates, of course, the blood also circulates the oxygen absorbed in the fine capillaries of the lungs. This ensures a more efficient and rapid distribution of blood (oxygen and nutrients) to all

Figure 4.5 Hazel nuts opened by animals

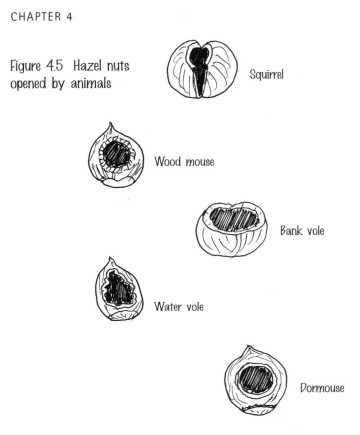

Squirrel

Wood mouse

Bank vole

Water vole

Dormouse

Figure 4.6.1 Alimentary tract of the rabbit

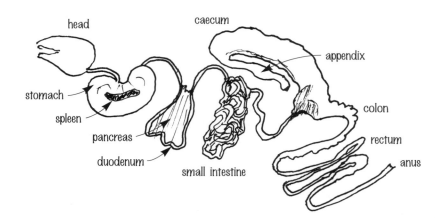

Figure 4.6.2 Alimentary tract of the cockroach

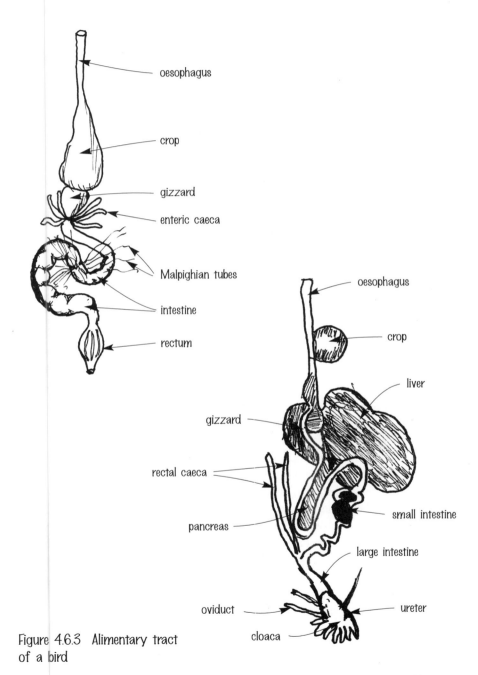

Figure 4.6.3 Alimentary tract
of a bird

parts of the body. In invertebrates, oxygen diffuses slowly through the blood and this is a major feature that effectively limits the size of, for example, insects.

Size in animals

A warm-blooded animal has to generate enough heat to maintain its characteristic body temperature and the energy that has to be used for this, which comes from the digested part of the food, is chiefly affected by the rate at which heat is lost.

Now, in general, the food intake is related to size – obviously, larger animals can eat more than small ones. (As with humans, there are exceptions!) But heat loss tends to be related to surface area and, in general, the smaller the animal, the greater the surface area relative to its weight. This is exactly the same for spheres, or cubes, or people. So food intake does not usually go up in strict proportion to size (but in relation to weight to the power of c. 0.75), and very small animals have to eat enormously to provide enough energy. Thus, if a shrew is deprived of food for even 12 hours, it will die, and, in consequence, such small animals have to eat every few hours, unless they hibernate (deliberately lowering body temperature and metabolic rate).

The need to maintain a relatively constant temperature, usually well above that of their surroundings, actually imposes lower limits on the size of warm-blooded animals (mammals and birds). So the smallest possible mammal is close to the weight of the pygmy shrew – 2.5–7.5 g, compared with 5–11 g for a harvest mouse and 40 g for a house mouse) and the smallest birds are certain species of hummingbirds (the wren weights about 5 g); there is a Cuban humming bird that measures only 2 cm (³/4 in) and has a heart rate of 1,000 beats per minute. Of course, heat loss also depends on degree of insulation, provided by fur, feathers, subcutaneous fat and nesting material, and ambient temperature. It may then be asked how the offspring of these small animals manage, especially since they are often hairless. The newly born pygmy shrew weighs no more than about 0.25 g !

There are three main answers: (1) they huddle together within an insulating nest, often incorporating fur, (2) they are kept warm by brooding adults and (3) they are provided with a good supply of high energy food (milk, insects, worms).

One consequence of small size is that animals can fall quite safely from quite a height without damaging themselves. Mice, ducklings emerging from holes used by tree-nesting ducks, even squirrels, simply drop to the ground and run off. Insects have less of a problem: grasshoppers and click beetles (which have a spring-loaded spike on their backs) simply fling themselves off into the air.

How animals 'see' the garden

When thinking about animals, it must not be supposed that they 'see' the world (the garden or their part of it) in the same way as we do. Clearly, very small animals will be unaware of the garden as a whole or even that there is such a thing. Others, capable of ranging widely (for example foxes and pheasants) may not recognize that the garden is in any way separate from the rest of their range. We cannot assume that this is so, however, and if a garden has a dog, or even a cat, other animals may recognize that boundaries exist.

Perhaps it is unimportant whether they are aware of the concept or not. The fact is that whatever they are aware of (a hedge, a flower, a leaf, the soil), they may sense it quite differently from the way we do. We rely heavily on sight and, though scent is important in a garden, our sense of smell is relatively poorly developed and other mammals and many insects use it far more effectively. We are so acutely aware of our reliance on sight that we underestimate, for example, our own sense of touch. We wonder how animals detect their prey or their food in muddy water: yet if we dropped a ring into a muddy pool, we would probably have little difficulty in finding it with our fingers – we would certainly try. There is a considerable dependence on recognition of an object – we already know what the ring feels like – but we can also identify objects of a general type (a twig as opposed to a stone). Even more commonly, we feel in our pockets daily and remove selected objects, distinguishing one coin from another and so on.

Our skin sensitivity is well-known but little thought about. We can feel the presence of a tiny insect (for example an aphid), just as we can detect very small rain droplets. A very good example of how we combine senses of hearing and touch is our behaviour in the close presence of a mosquito in the dark: it is even possible to kill it without seeing it.

Those animals with good vision do not always perceive colour and others (for example bees) respond to wavelengths that we do not. Most insects and birds, and some reptiles, can see the short-wave ultra-violet (UV) end of the spectrum, which we cannot. Markings on flowers that are only visible in UV light guide insects to the source of nectar, and spiders' webs may reflect UV light to serve as a lure to insects. Bats use their own echo-location and many insects and spiders are very sensitive to minute vibrations.

It is not really understood how some parasitic insects such as ichneumon flies can detect the larvae of others inside a tree trunk or branch and insert an egg inside them by drilling through several centimetres of wood. You only have to observe blackbirds and thrushes on a lawn to notice how they listen for earthworms before pouncing on them. Less well known is the way they will sometimes 'stamp' with their feet to attract earthworms to the surface (it is thought to imitate raindrops – how else would an earthworm know that it was raining on the surface?). This 'paddling' behaviour is more commonly seen in black-headed gulls on grassland.

Insect eyes are constructed quite differently from ours and such 'compound' eyes are particularly adapted to detecting movement across their field of vision. A fly's compound eye is a honeycomb of about 750 tiny lenses, each looking at a single part of the field of view. The eye is very lightweight but the fly is very good at detecting both motion and shape. The male is said to be able to track down a female in flight and land on it!

Taste is also much used to test and identify substrates, especially for herbivorous animals (for example leaf eaters, sap suckers).

The variety of animals and the way they use their senses is so great that it is only possible to recognize that they see things differently. It has always puzzled me that, while nearly all adult robins look alike to me, any male, for example, can, immediately and at some distance, recognize both its own mate and any strange male, the latter making it exhibit its well-known aggressive territorial behaviour.

5 What goes on in the Soil

In the soil is found a complex mixture of mineral particles (see Table 5.1), dead organic matter, soil water and dissolved salts, plant roots, seeds, microscopic plants and animals, larger invertebrates and some mammals. All these constituents are in a continual state of flux. Quite apart from the addition of fertilizers, water and other substances supplied by the gardener, the populations of organisms are changing all the time (with the season but for other reasons, too), all unknown and unseen from above the surface.

Table 5.1 Composition of a soil

Water		
Air		
Clay	Particle size:	0.002 mm
Silt		<0.05 mm
Sand		fine to coarse, 0.05–2.0 mm
Organic matter	humus	c. 40%
	cellulose and hemicellulose	c. 10%
	nitrogenous compounds	c. 35%
	resins, fats, waxes	
Main minerals	Nitrogen (N)	
	Phosphorus (P)	
	Potassium (K)	
	Calcium (Ca)	
	Magnesium (Mg)	
	Sulphur (S)	

Trace elements and micronutrients	Boron (B)
	Cadmium (Cd)
	Cobalt (Co)
	Copper (Cu)
	Nickel (Ni)
	Lead (Pb)
	Zinc (Zn)
	Selenium (Se)
	Iron (Fe)
	Molybdenum (Mo)
	Manganese (Mn)

A very good illustration of this process of change is the lifecycle of roots. We are all familiar with the continual renewal of leaves: old ones die off and fall to the ground and new ones develop, expand and often change colour. Exactly the same processes apply to roots. Of course, there are fairly permanent big structural roots, just as there may be long-lasting stems above ground, but there is also a continual growth and development of new roots exploring the soil and a simultaneous death of old ones, which contribute to the soil organic matter and thus to soil structure. Underneath the lawn, for example, an individual root lasts no longer than an individual grass leaf (that is, about six weeks).

Such vegetable matter is processed by small animals (detrivores – see Table 5.2), including earthworms (see Box 5.1), some of which also drag leaves down into the soil, and moved about by other burrowing animals (notably moles). So both soil-makers and soil-movers are involved in what goes on below the ground.

Soil-makers

This category includes any animal, such as an earthworm, that consumes the soil itself, digests and absorbs part of it and perhaps adds mucus by external secretion and as part of the undigested remnants and the products of metabolism in its faeces. These activities change the nature of the soil, creating, for example, humus. The sheer

Table 5.2 Typical detrivores

Primary decomposers

Bacteria
Beetles
Fungi
Fly larvae
Nematodes

Secondary decomposers

(of the droppings of the primary decomposers)

Earthworms
Springtails
Diptera (fly) larvae
Enchyrraeids (small worms)
Diplopods (pill millipedes)

Box 5.1 Earthworms

The 28 species, belonging to 8 genera, so far reported from the British Isles all belong to the family *Lumbricidae*, to which the large *Lumbricus terrestris* belongs. This is the worm that lives in deep burrows but surfaces at night to leave the well-known worm-cast on lawns. The amount of soil that such worms can move is enormous and has been variously calculated at 10–50 tonnes per ha (10–51 tons per 2^1/2 acres) per year, equivalent to raising the surface by 5 mm (^{1}/4 in) per year.

Earthworms are hermaphrodite but mate, lying alongside each other and facing in opposite directions. Their eggs are contained in cocoons, generally close to the surface between late spring and midsummer. They grow bigger over about three years and numbers vary with the site: under grass, numbers are probably of the order of 300–400 per 1 m^2 (1^1/4 sq yd). Their consumption of organic matter has been estimated at up to 25–30 tonnes (dry weight) per ha (20^1/4–30^1/2 tons per 2^1/2 acres) per year. The passage of soil through the earthworm aids the formation of humus.

Table 5.3 Soil organism

(numbers vary with soil type and cover, with more under grass, for example)

Common name	Latin name	Numbers
Springtails	*Collembola*	27,000 per m² (1^{1}/4 sq yd)
	(Total arthropods	260,000 per m²/1^{1}/4 sq yd)
Roundworms (eelworms)	*Nematoda*	20 million per m² (1^{1}/4 sq yd)
Mites	*Acarina*	10 million per m² (1^{1}/4 sq yd)
Earthworms	*Lumbricus* spp.	300,000 per ha (2^{1}/2 acres)

numbers of these organisms are extraordinary (see Table 5.3).

In addition to the detrivores, there are large numbers of carnivorous creatures, living on others in or on the soil. These, too, excrete their faeces into the soil and thus contribute to the processing that goes on all the time and in this case is probably less affected by ambient temperatures, since soil temperature varies much less at depth than at the surface and is protected from most weather conditions. Organisms that are not eaten must still die and their bodies are recycled by detrivores.

Excreta is an important component of soil but it does not all come from soil inhabitants. Considerable quantities may be derived from animals living above ground, eating the vegetation or preying on the herbivores, and also from dogs, cats and overflying birds. This material is dealt with by a variety of organisms (see Box 5.2) and without all this activity the soil would be inert, instead of the living complex in which plants thrive.

Soil movers

It is to this living soil that gardeners add fertilizer, lime, fine sand and compost, but it is worth recognizing that an army of mobile composters is already at work there. Many creatures move soil about in a minor

---

Box 5.2 Dung, droppings and distributors

Animal excreta, fortunately, disappears very quickly due to the action of birds, flinging it about in the search for insects; flies, which lay their eggs in the droppings, on which the emerging grubs feed, breaking it down quite rapidly; earthworms, which bury it, often dragging pieces below ground; and dung beetles, which also bury balls of dung, in which they lay their eggs.

The yellow dung fly (*Ceratophys typhoeus*) is an abundant scavenger, often seen in swarms on freshly deposited dung. The yellowish hairy-bodied males are rather more noticeable than the duller, greenish, non-hairy females.

The dung or dor beetle (*Geotrupes stercorarius*) (Table 4.1) is one of our biggest beetles and digs a tunnel over 50 cm (2 in) deep in which it buries a plug of dung as food for its larva. Like so many other creatures (for example bumble-bees and slugs) it is commonly infested with a tiny mite, which pierces the skin between its plates of mail and sucks its blood.

---

way – mining bees bring up small pyramids of soil, mainly in lawns or other undisturbed surfaces, and other insects make burrows – but the only animals that move soil in substantial quantities are rabbits, certain ants (especially the mound-forming small yellow ant *Acanthamyops flavus*), moles and earthworms (*Lumbricus* spp.).

Rabbits and ants will occur only in the wilder parts of gardens, and the former only in fairly large areas. The mounds formed by the yellow ant are often spectacular for such a small creature, often measuring 30 cm (12 in) in height and over 70 cm (2¼ ft) in length. They are characteristically oriented in an east-west direction, with the eastern end less sloping, so that they can actually be used as a compass!

Moles can occur anywhere and get rid of the soil removed in tunnelling by making molehills. The earth is pushed up in front of the mole by one front foot and ejected up a vertical shaft. This is often soil of a fine texture and can simply be removed for use elsewhere. However, moles also make shallow tunnels where the earth is simply raised up as a ridge. The mole patrols all these tunnels to eat the invertebrates that fall into them and while a great many pests may be consumed, including wireworms and leatherjackets, a lot of earthworms, which have many good attributes, are also eaten.

As Darwin observed (over more than 40 years, publishing his first paper on the subject in 1837), the amount of soil that earthworms can move is phenomenal. It is estimated that they bring up to the surface some 10 tonnes per ha (10 tons per 2½ acres) per year, raising the surface by 2.5 cm (1 in) every five years. Their effects on soil structure, drainage and aeration are considerable and they also attract many birds, especially to lawns. Blackbirds and thrushes are especially active, it taking a fairly substantial bird to drag a big earthworm out of its burrow. Robins will eat many earthworms and other soil organisms but generally either take them from the surface or accompany the biggest earth-mover to be found in gardens – the gardener.

It is surprising how many earthworms come to the surface of a lawn at night, provided it is damp. Since few birds are about in the dark, this is clearly a sensible strategy that also avoids sunlight and desiccation. However, foxes know about earthworms surfacing at night and there are times when worms contribute a surprisingly high proportion of their diet.

Recycling

Recycling can be done under the control of the gardener or by the activity in the soil described above, which plays a major role.

Controlled recycling

This is a familiar concept for gardeners which takes several forms. First, there are the methods of making compost, of both garden and organic household waste. These processes, of course, use the very same organisms that occur naturally: indeed, we rarely need to add any to our compost heaps. Long-lasting heaps and pits, as opposed to the relatively quick use of containers, develop their own flora and fauna and can deal with almost anything organic. The brandling worm (*Eisenia foetida*) may become very numerous in such composts.

For prunings and woody material, however, most gardeners make a bonfire. This only retains the mineral ash and the organic matter is destroyed. Leaving aside the pleasure that so many people appear to derive from stoking a bonfire and the beneficial effects it can have on the site used (unwanted nettles and brambles especially) and on pests and diseases, the bonfire is only useful if there is no better way of disposing of the material.

In a large garden, especially if there are wild or woodland areas, brushwood can be used to build up hedges, over which attractive creepers (for example honeysuckle) can be grown. These form good sites for hedgerow-nesting birds, such as blackbirds, thrushes, robins and hedge-sparrows. Such hedges gradually subside as the wood rots away and more can be added almost continuously.

Natural recycling

The incorporation of leaf litter by earthworms has already been mentioned, but what about the remains of animals? Small animals are present in vast numbers but tend to have surprisingly short lives (see Table 5.4). This is true for many of our garden birds and mammals, so the number of dead bodies must be substantial – yet we rarely encounter any of them. This is partly because predators such as foxes are also quite prepared to consume dead animals and partly because there are a number of carrion eaters to remove the corpses. Crows (full name carrion crow) and magpies perform this useful service – as they do on roads, removing crushed hedgehogs, for example. Such birds typically have heavy bills (see Box 1.2). Unpleasant as it may seem to us, their activities help to keep our world clean and tidy.

Table 5.4 Longevity of animals

(The figures given are those for the survivors – the ones seen in a garden: early mortality can be very high and averages mean very little.)

Mammals	Typical life-span
Squirrel	up to 6 years
Fox	up to 8 years
Rabbit	up to 8 years
Vole	<15 months
House mouse	<18 months
Rat	<18 months
Shrew	c. 1 year

Mammals	Typical life-span	
Bat	c. 4 years	

Birds		
Robin	c. 1 year	
Blackbird	<2 years	
Swallow	up to 15 years	
Wren	c. 1 year	
Pigeon	c. 2 years	

Amphibians		
Frog	up to 12 years	Tadpole 2–5 months
Newt	c. 4 years (up to 20 years)	Newtpole 3.5–4 months
Toad	up to 40 years	

Reptiles		
Grass snake	4–5 years	
Slow worm	up to 30 years (one recorded at 54 years!)	

Invertebrates	Adult	Larva
Butterfly	<1 year	some weeks or up to 1 year
Bumble-bee	queen <1 year worker 2–3 months	<2 weeks
Wasp	queen c. 1 year worker 2–3 months	4–6 weeks
Honey-bee	queen 2–3 years active worker 6 weeks	c. 3 weeks
Mayfly	<1 day	c. 1 year
Dragonfly	4–8 weeks	1–2 years
Crane-fly	2–3 days	c. 11 months
Ants	queen >5 years	
Snail	2–3 (up to 10) years	
Earthworm	up to 6 years	

If bodies are not removed in this way they may be buried, and this may happen quite quickly. Burying beetles (*Necrophorus* spp.), for example, will dig away the earth beneath a carcase until it sinks down out of sight (sometimes in as little as 12 hours). They do this to provide food for their progeny and lay their eggs on the buried body.

If bodies remain on the surface for even a short period they will be visited by blowflies (for example the greenbottle, *Lucilia* spp. and the bluebottle, *Calliphora* spp.) which will lay their eggs on the carcass and, when these hatch, the resulting maggots will simply consume the corpse. They form a rather revolting mass of seething grubs which, when fully grown, simply burrow down into the earth beneath and pupate.

Soil phases of pests

Quite apart from the creatures so far mentioned, a great many that spend most of their active lives on plants, often as pests, have a phase in the soil. In orchards, for example, several prominent pests are of this type. The caterpillars of the apple sawfly, which feed on fruitlets, leave the fruit in early to midsummer and drop to the ground, where they form cocoons at a depth of 8–24 cm (3^{1}/8–9^{1}/2 in). These cocooned larvae overwinter in this phase and pupate in early spring, the adults emerging in time to lay their eggs on the new crop of apples. The pear and cherry slugworm (larvae of the pear and cherry sawfly) has a similar life cycle. Apple and pear midges, similarly, have an over-wintering larval phase in the soil, following the last of the 3–4 generations that occur in the summer.

Winter moth females are wingless and crawl up tree trunks to lay their 100–200 eggs in bark crevices. When the larvae are ready to pupate, just before midsummer, they drop to the ground and bury themselves within the top 10 cm (4 in). These pupae may be vulnerable to attack by ground beetles or parasitic nematodes, so biological control of pests can be exercised (see Chapter 7). Carnivorous larvae of ground beetles will feed on such pupae or larvae throughout the winter, unless temperatures are very low.

Fungi in the soil

Apart from their fruiting bodies, in the form of mushrooms and toadstools – which appear above ground – nothing is usually seen of the fungal species present in the soil (mycorrhizal fungi), yet they are there in large quantities and have several functions. They break down organic matter and thus contribute to recycling, being especially important in wood; they may trap and destroy pests (see Box 5.3); and they associate closely with plant roots and aid plant nutrition (see Box 5.4).

Box 5.3 Fungi in biological control

Fungus	Organism controlled
Verticillium lecanii	Aphids
Metarhizium flavoviride (a mycorrhizal fungus, see Box 5.4)	Vine weevil on strawberry and blackcurrant
Zoophthora radicans	Diamond-back moth on vegetable crops

Box 5.4 Mycorrhizal fungi

The word 'mycorrhiza' means 'fungus root' and it refers to a symbiotic relationship between a particular fungus and the roots of a particular plant species (some fungi, however, associate with many species). Some grow inside the roots, while others are mainly found on the outside.

As in all symbiotic relationships, both partners benefit, and many of these fungi cannot grow in the absence of a host plant. The main benefits to the plant are more efficient uptake and utilization of soil nutrients, but there is also greater tolerance of environmental stress and of diseases. Indeed, it has recently been found that some diseases are suppressed (in ways not yet understood) by the presence of mycorrhiza. This is so for tomatoes grown hydroponically, where the addition of the mycorrhiza fungus *Glomus intraradices* leads to suppression of phytophthora root rot. This is most useful in growing media that are sterile and have no natural mycorrhiza.

6 Seasonal Change

Seasonal patterns, of course, have an enormous influence on everything in the garden. All gardeners recognize, and try to exploit, the seasons, planting species that will provide a succession of flowers and foliage at most times of the year.

Midwinter

Midwinter is a challenge and visible plant life slows or even appears to stop. Not entirely, however, and growth can be found if it is sought (depending, of course, on the severity of the winter.)

The buds of trees can be detected at the beginning of winter and cell multiplication takes place in preparation for the rapid extension that occurs in the spring. Deciduous trees can be distinguished and identified in the winter by their buds and their bark (see Box 6.1). Other plants adopt different strategies for surviving harsh weather conditions and ensuring the capacity to grow again when the temperature rises.

Annuals normally produce seed, with varying amounts of reserves (mainly of starch) which can be drawn upon to grow the initial shoots, leaves and roots. Seeds are astonishingly resistant to cold, heat and drying, but they may be eaten (even then sometimes passing through the gut of birds and mammals undamaged) or destroyed by fungal attack. Many remain dormant in the soil for many years; some, such as acorns, are buried as food stores for the winter by jays and grey squirrels (but not red squirrels, which cannot digest them), and not all of these are recovered.

Perennials also produce seed, to generate new individuals, but each plant also adapts to winter conditions: in deciduous trees, the loss of leaves is a means of reducing exposure to frost, heavy snow and high winds. In most of the UK, temperatures do not stay very low for long

Box 6.1 Buds and bark of deciduous trees

Tree	Latin name	Bark	Buds
Alder	*Alnus glutinosa*	Dark grey with fissures	Purplish-brown, club-shaped, narrow at base, set alternately along dark brown twigs
Ash	*Fraxinus excelsior*	Pale grey and smooth	Hard, black in pairs, except 3 at tip
Beech	*Fagus sylvatica*	Smooth grey	Long, pointed, brown
Cherry	*Prunus avium*	Purplish brown with metallic lustre	Large, oval, pointed, red-brown
Elm	*Ulmus* spp.	Grey, cracked into small squares	Small, rounded, green tinged with red
Hawthorn	*Crataegus monogyna*	Orange-brown, cracking	Short, stumpy and dark brown, borne on short stems
Hazel	*Corylus* spp.	Mottled grey and brown, smooth	Female catkins are bud-shaped with tufts of crimson stigmas, otherwise buds are smooth and green
Horse chestnut	*Aesculus hippocastanum*	Red-brown or grey, scaly	Big, brown buds, sticky in spring
Lime	*Tilea x europaea*	Grey brown with shallow fissures	Only 2 visible outer scales, 1 larger than the other
Oak	*Quercus robur*	Pale grey and fissured	Many-scaled, pale brown, oval
Silver birch	*Betula pendula*	White with dark rugged cracks at the base	Small, slender, pointed and diverge from twigs

Sweet chestnut	*Castanea sativa*	Grey and smooth, spirally ringed with age	Singly-set, oval
Sycamore	*Acer pseudoplatanus*	Pinkish to yellowish grey, some peeling	Hard, green, paired except for terminal buds at shoot tip
Willow	*Salix fragilis*	Dark grey, deeply fissured	Oval, pointed on yellow shoots

Buds of hawthorn (in early spring)

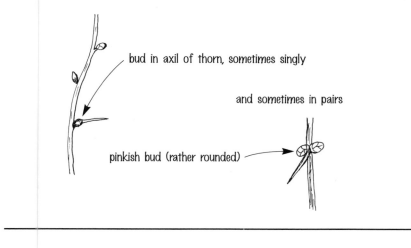

bud in axil of thorn, sometimes singly

and sometimes in pairs

pinkish bud (rather rounded)

---

periods and some plant growth will occur whenever the temperature allows. Grasses will grow as soon as the temperature rises above about 4°C (39°F), for example.

Animals also vary in the way they adapt to winter conditions: the most extreme adaptations are hibernation and migration to areas with more suitable climatic conditions (see Chapter 10). Cold-blooded creatures, such as snakes, frogs, toads and newts, hide away in holes, protected hedge-bottoms or, in the case of frogs, in the mud at the bottom of ponds and ditches. Their metabolism falls with decreasing temperature, so they do not need food; they simply have to avoid freezing. Fish do this by keeping to deeper water and many aquatic insects and crustaceans do the same, but some, such as *Daphnia* and *Cyclops* (see Chapter 9) actually thrive at quite low temperatures and their populations are often highest in late winter.

Some insects 'hibernate' (see Table 6.1) but this is simply total inactivity at low temperatures. Hibernation proper, as occurs in some mammals (but not birds), involves a marked drop in body temperature and in metabolic rate resulting in a deep torpor (see Table 6.2). However, very few British mammals actually hibernate: squirrels, rabbits, foxes, most mice, rats, moles, voles and shrews do not, though they may rest for a few days in their winter nests during very harsh weather.

Table 6.1 Examples of 'hibernating' insects

Butterflies	9 species as eggs, 35 as larvae and 7 as adults (e.g. brimstone, Camberwell beauty, comma, tortoiseshells)
Ladybirds	2-spot ladybirds (*Adalis bipunctata*) congregate in numbers (50 or more) to 'hibernate' under bark or even in houses
Cluster-flies (*Pollenia rudis*)	Behave in the same way as 2-spot ladybirds, often in lofts or disused rooms
Lacewing flies (e.g. *Chrysopa carnea*)	The green lacewing 'hibernates' in houses, sheds etc. and changes to a reddish colour, changing back to green in the spring

Table 6.2 Hibernating mammals

	Body temperature
Hedgehog	Normal 34°C (93°F); hibernation 4–6°C (39–43°F)
Dormouse	Feels cold to the touch and the external temperatures may be close to ambient (but not freezing): internal temperatures are higher
Bats	Length of hibernation may be mid-autumn to early spring, 6–12°C (43–54°F°), depending on the species

Insect populations generally fall markedly during the winter. Some insects overwinter as pupae (for example many butterflies), and some as eggs. Some, in protected situations (such as stage beetle larvae within rotten logs), remain active where they are. Other insects may remain fairly numerous but are less active and less obvious: this is the case for some ants (for example the black lawn ant), of which workers may live for several years, or underground-dwelling ants (for example the yellow lawn ant), but in others (for example the large black ant) the workers do not seem to live for more than a season. The main garden ants are listed in Table 6.3.

Table 6.3 Garden ants

Common name	Latin name	Nest site	Food
Black lawn or garden ant	*Lasius niger*	On the lawn or around the house foundations	Secretions of greenflies etc., insects
Common red ant	*Myrmica rubra*	Small colonies under stones or in low thyme-covered mounds	Insects and other small creatures
Yellow lawn ant	*Lasius mixtus*	Underground long tunnels (1 m/3^1/4 ft +)	Exudations of subterranean aphids
Yellow hill ant	*Lasius flavus*	Large earth mounds oriented E-W	Exudations of subterranean aphids

For many animals and plants the winter is a period of relative dormancy, with some in a state of suspended animation while others struggle to survive against harsh weather, low temperatures and scarce food supplies – though water is not usually a problem except where temperatures drop very low. It is somewhat surprising, therefore, to realize that many mammals are actually pregnant during this time and the foetus is, of course, actively growing. Birds are able

Table 6.4 Gestation in mammals

Species	Length of gestation (days)	Mating	Dates of birth
Fallow deer *Dama dama*	230	mid to late autumn	early to midsummer
Roe deer *Capreolus capreolus*	144 (post-implantation)	mid to late summer (implantation of egg delayed until early winter)	mid to late spring
Badger *Meles meles*	49 (post-implantation)	mainly late winter to late spring (implantation of egg may be delayed 3–10 months)	mid to late winter
Fox *Vulpes vulpes*	52–53	mid to late winter	early to mid-spring
Rabbit *Oryctolagus cuniculus*	28–33	any time of year	most litters born late winter to late summer
Hedgehog *Erinaceus europaeus*	31–35	mid-spring to late summer (after hibernation)	late spring onwards
Field vole *Microtus agrestis*	18–20	mainly mid-spring	mainly late spring
Wood mouse *Apodemus sylvaticus*	19–20	early spring to early autumn	mid-spring to mid-autumn
Common shrew *Sorex araneus*	20	early spring onwards	mid-spring to late summer
Common pipistrelle bat *Pipistrellus pipistrellus*	44–80	late summer to late autumn (sperm stored until fertilization in mid-spring)	early to midsummer

to mate just before breeding in the spring but for mammals to produce their young in early spring may require mating much earlier. This is most marked in larger mammals with long pregnancy periods but does not present the same problem for small mammals. These differences are illustrated in Table 6.4. Thus deer have 'rutting' seasons in the autumn and foxes can be heard engaged in mating activities during winter nights.

However, although birds do not start their courtship and mating activities until the spring, they can often be observed exploring nest sites during the winter (and even in late autumn). This is only noticeable for birds that nest in holes, but who knows whether hedge- or ground-nesting birds behave similarly or not? After all, how would you tell?

Spring

Although we usually recognize four main seasons, we all know that they are not sharply delineated and, in different years, may start early or finish late. So spring is a variable feast but, when it comes, it gives an impression of maximum biological activity. Light, temperature and moisture – the main determinants of plant growth – are usually adequate and many plants grow rapidly.

Tree and shrub buds burst but maximum shoot growth tends to be much later. This is very well illustrated by, for example, blackberry bushes. Leaves and flowers appear in the spring and berries in the later summer/autumn period: but the astounding shoot growth, often in the form of thick, green, fairly succulent leaders that trail over the ground for over 3 m (10 ft), occurs from early to late summer. Eventually these shoots make contact with the ground and then develop a clump of roots that will initiate a new bush at some distance from the old one, and in this way large areas can be colonized quite quickly.

The earliest growth often comes from plants with food reserves, in corms, bulbs, thick rhizomes or substantial tap-roots, making growth less dependent on current photosynthesis. Early flowers on trees and shrubs are often wind-pollinated, since there may be relatively few pollinating insects about that early. Catkins are a good example (such as hazel, birch, alder, hornbeam, oak, willow), bearing the male flowers so that the pollen is exposed to the wind, whereas the females flowers tend to be smaller and inconspicuous (see Figure 6.1). Grass generally grows at its most rapid rate in late spring but most grasses flower somewhat later (see page 71) and are wind-pollinated.

Figure 6.1 Flowers of wind-pollinated trees

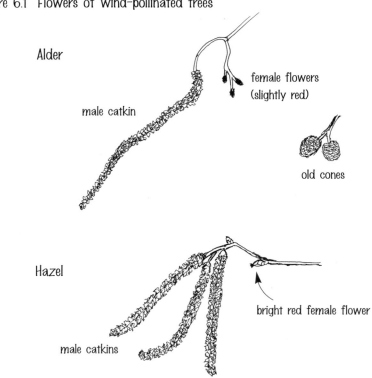

Alder

male catkin

female flowers (slightly red)

old cones

Hazel

male catkins

bright red female flower

Those plants that make early growth from their reserves need to replenish them during the summer, so it is important that they retain their leaves after flowering in order to build up their bulbs, rhizomes or tap-roots for the next spring. This is so for daffodils and bluebells, for example, even though the foliage may not look very attractive: some gardeners interplant with other species that provide an attractive display to cover the gently senescing bulb leaves.

During the spring, there is vast reproductive activity by plants (except for fungi), birds, mammals, some insects, amphibians and a host of other animals. They all produce many more potential progeny than are needed to replace the often substantial winter losses and to maintain the population. This is particularly so for plants and insects that provide no parental care: losses too are on a vast scale and, were it not so, populations would reach plague or pest proportions, exhaust their food supplies and die of starvation and/or disease. As it is, other species of animals live on the surplus and, in this way, the balance of nature is maintained. Much the same applies to amphibians.

Birds, mammals, some insects and spiders, however, do provide parental care. In the first two the burden of pregnancy and egg production, and the further burden of feeding the young, limit the number of offspring to something nearer what is needed for replacement. This is particularly so for larger mammals and birds, but these may also live longer, and this reduces the needed annual replacement rate.

Those insects and spiders, such as earwigs and wolf spiders, that do provide some parental care (see Box 4.4), may nonetheless produce large numbers of small eggs, since small creatures are more vulnerable to losses than are big ones. Many of these small creatures actually reproduce to a greater extent in the summer.

Summer

Depending on regional variation, summer tends to be much drier, with higher temperatures and higher evaporation rates. It is not always appreciated that the water balance results from rainfall minus the evaporation and that the latter is similar (per unit area) for a complete vegetation cover and for an open water surface, being more related to the evaporative 'pull' (capacity) of the ambient atmosphere than to anything else. The resulting balance is often negative: for example, in the south-east of England there can be a deficit of 15 cm (6 in) of rainfall over the summer period. As a consequence, the water table can fall dramatically (see Box 6.2).

Box 6.2 The water table

The water table refers to the underlying reservoir of water, which may be at a considerable depth and, in these circumstances, may not have much effect at the soil surface. On low-lying land, however, it may even appear above the surface of the lowest land, forming pools or lakes in the winter that dry out in the summer.

The water level can rise and fall spectacularly, at many times the depth of rainfall. If 2.5 cm (1 in) of rain falls on a pond the level will rise by approximately that amount, but the same amount of rain on soil may cause much bigger changes in the water table since the water is dispersed among crevices between the soil particles and can therefore saturate a much greater depth of soil. Thus 2.5 cm (1 in) of rainfall may saturate as much as 15 cm (6 in) of soil (varying with the soil type) and, if this contributes to the water table (where this is high enough to be affected), it may thus rise by several times as much as the rainfall depth.

Even if the water-table is too deep to be involved, the same principle applies during a drought. Thus a loss of 2.5 cm (1 in) by evaporation from the vegetation can dry out soil to a depth of 15 cm (6 in). That is why the soil can often appear so dry to so great a depth during the summer.

Many creatures that feed on plants derive all the moisture they need from their food, since most plants have a very high water content (see Table 6.5). Similarly, animals that eat other animals may do the same, since animal bodies also contain a high percentage of water. Where they do not, as in the chitinous wing-cases of beetles, for example, these are simply discarded or voided in the faeces. Those that do need to drink may be able to use dew-laden vegetation but during very dry periods may become highly dependent on lakes, ponds and puddles. Bees, wasps and butterflies that may not be about when dew is available may use fruit, nectar or, in sharp contrast, fresh dung, as a source of moisture.

All animals have to maintain a water balance just as warm-blooded animals have to try to maintain a near-constant temperature, but there are probably more ways of adjusting temperature (by the use of shade, burrows, body posture, nests and so on) than there are of controlling water balance. Cold-blooded animals have less of a problem with both, and small ones especially can easily seek out

Table 6.5 Water content of plants

(depends on stage of growth)

Species	% of water in fresh material*
Clover (*Trifolium* spp.)	85–89
Perennial ryegrass (*Lolium perenne*)	85 (c. 60% in midsummer)
Cocksfoot (*Dactylis glomerata*)	82 (c. 56% in midsummer)
Cabbage	88
Broccoli	89
Brussels sprouts	87
Mushroom (*Agaricus bisporus*)	89–91
Cucumber (as eaten)	96
Tomatoes (as eaten)	93

* Such figures always refer to above-ground parts of the plant (chemical composition data also normally ignore the roots).

relatively humid environments (for example under logs and stones).

Insects and spiders thrive in the summer but, of course, so do their predators. Food is generally plentiful for most animals and populations increase.

Autumn

Animals rely on heavy feeding in the autumn to see them through the following winter. Fortunately for those that feed on them, seeds and fruit are usually in considerable surplus at this time. Sometimes, this reveals the presence of animals that are otherwise unseen.

For example, from late summer, hazelnuts are big enough for mammals to collect or consume. If they are collected, of course, you may simply notice that they have gone (as may happen with many nuts, such as walnuts). However, quite often they are eaten and the empty shells are left behind. In that case it is often possible to tell who has eaten them, because they open the shells (for example of hazelnuts) in different ways in order to extract the kernel (see Figure 4.5). The differences, which can be very marked, include features such as the toothmarks made by wood mice but not by voles. Half-chewed rose hips, vetch seed pods and the remains of sycamore seeds are left about by voles, sometimes close to their nests or tunnels.

The most spectacular autumnal changes are certainly in the vegetation. Prior to the loss of leaves in deciduous trees, there is often a marked change in their colour. This is largely due to the withdrawal of useful compounds from the leaf, so that there is less wastage to the tree (especially of protein) when the leaves fall off. Red colours are revealed by the withdrawal of green chlorophyll, for example.

The fallen leaves are not wasted in the whole biological system. All kinds of minute animals (detrivores) feed on them, just as earthworms do if they fall on grassy areas. They may also provide the medium for fungal growth, most of which is also more noticeable and spectacular in the autumn. This is mainly due to the appearance of fruiting bodies such as mushrooms and toadstools, which most people think of as 'the fungi'. This is a bit like regarding the apple as the species/individual rather than the tree. The purpose of the fruiting bodies is to produce vast numbers of minute spores above ground, where they can be spread by wind to colonize other sites. Very often, these fruiting bodies are quite short-lived. Puffballs (*Lycoperdon* spp.), for example, illustrate this very well. They appear as small, fairly hard, button-like bodies, which swell up rapidly into easily burst, papery balls, full of millions of minuscule spores. The latter appear simply as a yellow-brown cloud when the balls are burst.

The main part of the fungus, growing unseen in rotting wood or the soil whenever conditions permit (dampness is essential but they easily survive drought), is a great mass of filamentous threads, the hyphae. Sometimes these may form quite broad, flat, strap-like structures, well seen beneath the bark of an elm killed off by Dutch elm disease. The fine threads may also be parasitic on living plants, causing plant diseases, but the toadstools are generally saprophytes (living on decaying organic matter), breaking down leaves, twigs and whole tree stumps: they are a vital part of recycling.

Above: Plate 1. Rose leaves with pieces cut out by leaf-cutter bees.

Left: Plate 2. Common fritillary beside a pond covered in duckweed.

Right: Plate 3. A group of water-side plants in mid-spring with common forget-me-not and kingcup (or marsh marigold) at the centre, loddon lily behind, lungwort to the right and primrose below. The sword-like leaves of water iris (yellow flag) are visible but it is too early for flowers.

Above left: Plate 4. Cleavers or 'goose-grass', showing the small stem connecting leaves to root.
Above right: Plate 5. Lungwort used as ground cover.
Below: Plate 6. Loddon lilies growing by the pond.

Above: Plate 7. Dustbin lids in position.

Below: Plate 8. Vole departing.

Above: Plate 9. Two Grass snakes mating.

Below: Plate 10. Nest of long-tailed field mouse.

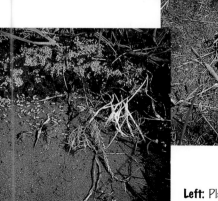

Left: Plate 11. Black ants' nest.

Above: Plate 12. Grass snake swimming in the pond.

Above: Plate 13. Lily leaves showing pieces cut out by China mark moth larvae.

Above left: Plate 14. Libellula dragonfly and the larval case from which it emerged.
Left: Plate 15. School pond to show construction.

Above left: Plate 16. 'Bedeguar' or 'Robin's pincushion' gall on a rose bush.

Above right: Plate 17. Marble galls on oak in winter.

Below left: Plate 18. Mallard duck sitting on nest in willow cleft.

Below right: Plate 19. Green woodpecker hole reduced by nuthatches using mud.

Above: Plate 20. Rabbit hole.

Above: Plate 21. Fox hole.

Below: Plate 22. Badger hole.

Below: Plate 23. Holes of the solitary bee *Andrena*

Right: Plate 24. Hole of a mining bee in a brick path.

Left: Plate 25. Wasps' nest in loft opened (Plate 26 above) to show pillars supporting layers of cells.

Above: Plate 27. Red ants' nest – mound covered in thyme but surrounded by periwinkle.

Top: Plate 28. Mallard nest on bank by pond, eggs uncovered for sitting on and (Plate 29, above) covered.

Right: Plate 30. Mallard eggs in tree cleft.

Above: Plate 32. Jackdaw arriving at the chimney with nesting material.

Above: Plate 31. Magpies' nest, with roof.

Above: Plate 33. The first three baby coots to hatch. The nest is on an island of branches and rushes.

Right: Plate 34. Owl box, disguised with bark, in position on a weeping willow tree. Plate 35. Baby grey squirrels in the owl box.

It is hard to see the fungal threads but their presence is often indicated by the pattern of fruiting bodies. For example, the fairy-ring fungus (*Marasmius oreades*), which produces rings of delicate, pinkish toadstools on lawns, does so because the original spore-infection has radiated hyphae in all directions which eventually fruit at their ends. The centre of the ring becomes exhausted of the material they feed on, so the hyphae die out, often producing a flush of dark green grass, so it is easy to visualize the network of threads that must have existed to create the toadstool rings.

Other fungi (mycorrhiza) form beneficial associations with roots (see Box 5.4), increasing the availability of minerals, such as phosphate, to some tree species (for example beech, oak, birch and pine). In some cases, the association is so close that no growth will occur in the absence of the right fungus – as in orchids. This is because the orchid seed is exceedingly small and takes years to develop into a plant. During this time, it depends upon these mycorrhizal fungi, which are saprophytes, to provide the carbohydrates which the orchid uses to grow and develop. Thus the orchid seedling, without green leaves but unable to live on dead plant material, uses the fungus to feed it. This is possible because part of the fungus is outside the seedling, living on humus, and passes the carbohydrates thus formed to that part of the fungus that lives inside the seedling and thence to the seedling itself.

This arrangement is all the more necessary since it may be up to three years before leaves appear and some of the orchids take up to 15 years to flower. Eventually, orchids may become free of the fungus (no longer needing it), but this is not so for all species. In many, the plant dies after flowering once or twice, so the infected, juvenile period is a substantial proportion of the life of the plant. No wonder they produce such vast numbers of their very small seeds.

Variable life-cycles

Although the division of the seasons into four has its uses, it is a rather crude way of looking at living things. As gardeners well know, plant life-cycles do not always fit this time frame, and the same is true for many animal species.

Snails, for example, will behave in much the same way during a very dry summer as they do when they hibernate in winter. They seal themselves up inside their shells (called 'aestivation' in dry times) and wait for conditions to improve. Birds may start breeding in the spring but, depending on the weather and food supplies, may repeat the process more than once during the summer. Newts usually arrive at water to breed in the spring but, in a very mild season, they can be found in late autumn.

So, as anyone who keeps a diary will find, there is a great variation in when things happen and what plants and animals can be found at particular times. Furthermore, some animals can only be found easily over quite short periods when they are especially engaged in certain activities. For example, wolf spiders can easily be seen carrying their egg sacs about, but perhaps only over a couple of weeks. Then suddenly their web-tents appear (often in early summer) in considerable numbers, in long grass without shade, but, a few weeks later, it may be difficult to find any trace of them. Observation of natural history is often very chancy and frequency of looking seems much more likely to reward the observer, whatever the season.

7 Ecology

Ecology is usually defined as the study of organisms in relation to their environment, but that is what all natural history is about and, in any case, raises the question of how the environment is defined. Albert Einstein said, 'The environment is everything that is not me!', which makes it a rather large subject. Furthermore, much of the environment would appear to be common to all species – but different parts of it are significant for different plants and animals and, for most species, it is only the local environment that matters. A species may be distributed world-wide but most individuals interact with only a small part of the world and, even within that, only a limited number of features play a central role in their lives.

Thus whales cover thousands of miles of ocean but know nothing of the land; migratory birds also cover vast distances but view most of the areas only from a considerable height. By contrast, an earthworm may be confined to a few cubic metres of soil and an oak tree remains rooted to the same place for its whole life. Of course, that does not mean that their environment is constant. The weather changes, moisture content and the nature of the air vary, other organisms, including people, come and go, and seasons change.

Indeed, although an oak tree is fixed, plenty of air travels past it and it is out of the carbon dioxide in the air that most of the tree is made. Here is a quick calculation: suppose the tree presents a circular cross-section from all aspects, like a spherical lollipop. The radius of the lolly might be 10 m (33 ft), with a cross-section of about 600 m^2 (6458 sq ft). If we imagine average speeds of 10 m (33 ft) per second, then the stationary oak samples 6000 m^3 (211,875 cu ft) of air per second. That is about 260,000 m^3 (9,181,270 cu ft) per day: not bad for a stationary object.

So the ecology of a species has to focus on those parts of the environment that are important to that species and this will include many other species and other individuals of the same species. Most species thus have a habitat that will contain the environmental features that are of significance to it, and, in some cases, this will be characterized by other individuals of the same, or particular different, species. These groups of organisms form associations, communities and colonies, and although these terms often have overlapping definitions there are some useful distinctions to be made.

Associations

If species are 'associated' with each other, some interaction is implied, but it falls short of specialized relationships such as parasitism or symbiosis (see later). Three examples of this will illustrate the concept: (1) bees and flowers; (2) elm trees and elm bark beetles; (3) blue tits and oak trees.

Bees and flowers

Bees collect both nectar and pollen from flowers and, in doing so, pollinate them (but only, of course, at the appropriate season). Flowers vary greatly in their structure and in the devices they have evolved for ensuring that when bees are taking nectar they actually get dusted with pollen in such a way that they will deliver it to another flower of the same species (see Box 7.1). Clearly, this would be an inefficient process if the insects went from one species to another: this suggests some advantage in plants forming large masses of the same species.

Different species of bee are associated with different flowers, mainly because a different length of 'tongue' is needed to reach the nectaries of different plants (see Box 7.2). Bumble-bees, of which there are about nine common species in the UK, vary in size, colour and tongue length but, in general, their tongues are much longer than those of honey-bees. Both bumble-bees and honey-bees live in colonies (see page 139) but there are also many species of solitary bees that serve as pollinators – some important enough to be used in agriculture (for example the alfalfa leaf-cutter bee, *Megachile rotundaba*, and the alkali bee, *Nomia melanderi*, used to pollinate alfalfa in the United States).

Box 7.1 Pollination by bees

Bees seek nectar and, in doing so, receive a dusting of pollen, mainly on the back of the thorax, which they transfer to the style and stigma (female organs) of the next flower they visit. This can be illustrated by looking at the structure of the common white dead nettle.

Structure of white dead-nettle flower

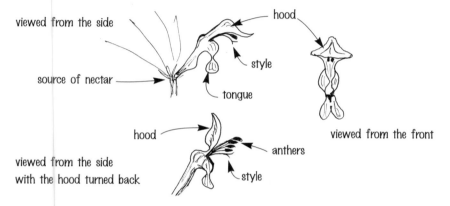

The bee lands on the 'tongue' and pushes forward into the flower to get at the nectar, which is at the bottom of the tubular flower stem. In doing this, the hood is pulled down, so that the pollen carried by the bee is transferred to the stigma. As the bee withdraws it receives another dusting of pollen from the anthers.

The foxglove is another, rather spectacular example.

Foxglove flower

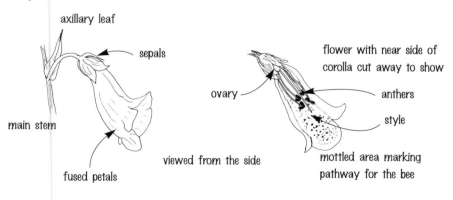

Box 7.2 Bumble-bee tongue lengths

Common British bumble-bees	Colour	Length of tongue (mm)*	Nest site
Bombus terrestris	Black with 2 yellow bands and a whitish rump	8.2	U
Bombus lucorum	Similar to above but paler yellow bands and pure white hind end	7.2	U
Bombus hortorum	As above but 3 yellow bands	13.5	S
Bombus lapidarius	Black with orange-red extremity	8.1	U
Bombus pratorum	As B. lucorum but smaller and with pale orange rump	7.1	S/U
Bombus pascuorum	Small, tawny yellow or brown all over	8.6	S

* 25 mm = 1 in

U: nest in holes in the ground

S: grassy/mossy nest above ground

Much-favoured flowers are *Antirrhinum* spp. and *Aconitum* spp. but different species favour different plants.

Elm trees and elm bark beetles

Although there are three main species quite widely distributed, the elm tree (family *Ulmaceae*) used to be regarded as typical of England particularly. However, vast numbers were destroyed in the major outbreak of Dutch elm disease in the early 1970s and, although new trees develop from suckers (since fertile seed is rarely produced), they tend to become infected after about 20 years. In the United States, Dutch elm disease was introduced from Europe in the 1930s.

The elm bark beetle (*Scolytus destructor*) tends to fly only at relatively high temperatures (about 26°C/79°F)), so trees are infested during hot spells. The beetles lay their eggs under the bark of the tree and

Figure 7.1 Elm bark beetles

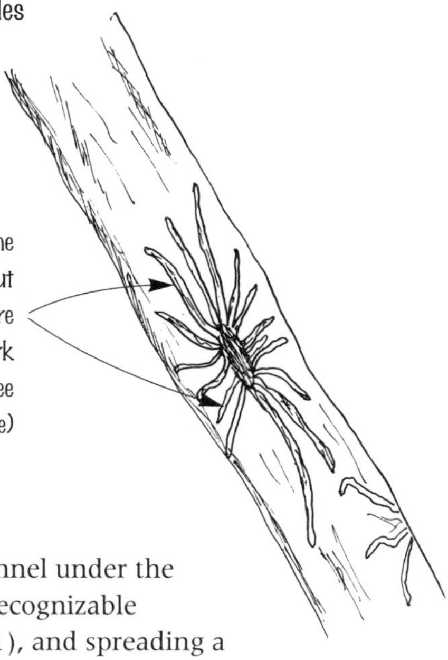

tunnels of the larvae of the
elm bark beetle radiating out
from where the eggs were
laid (drawn after the bark
had dropped off the treee
and the beetles long gone)

the emerging larvae tunnel under the
bark, radiating out in recognizable
patterns (see Figure 7.1), and spreading a
fungus (*Ceratostomella ulmi*) which eventually
destroys the water-carrying tissues (the xylem) and kills the tree,
which dies off from the top or from the ends of branches during the
summer. In a tree so killed, not only can the tunnelling be observed
as the bark falls away but the dried sheets of fungus can also easily be
seen. The fungus also has a characteristic smell.

Blue tits and oak trees

Blue tits tend to have large families, laying up to 14 eggs in a clutch.
The problem of feeding the developing nestlings is therefore
considerable and it is essential that the nest is within easy reach of a
major food supply. Commonly, this is the caterpillars which feed on
the first growth of oak leaves, in such numbers that they may greatly
reduce the foliage and the oak then produces a second crop of leaves.
Incidentally, the oak is said to be more persistently attacked by insects
than any other tree: it has been estimated that up to 500 different
species live on one part or another.

It seems that blue tits actually time their breeding (controlled by
the male) so that the nestlings hatch at the same time as certain
caterpillars start feeding on the oak leaves. Several species seem to be

involved, including the purple hair-streak (*Quercusia quercus*) and the green oak-roller (*Tortrix viridana*). Sparrow-hawks – which often feed on young blue tits – also adjust their breeding season to fit their need for food for their offspring to the emergence of young blue tits from the nest. This is yet another illustration of the point made in both the Chinese proverb, 'The mantis stalks the cicada, unaware of the yellow bird behind,' and the Ethiopian proverb, 'The eye of the leopard is on the goat, and the eye of the goat is on the leaf.'

Communities

None of the above examples could be held to involve communities. These are usually defined as social groupings within a circumscribed area, including assemblages of interacting species, with some degree of permanence. Three examples of communities are: (1) ants and aphids; (2) rotten logs; (3) flower beds.

Ants and aphids
Aphids (greenfly and blackfly) are sap-sucking insects that are very vulnerable to attack by numerous predators including birds, ladybirds and their larvae, and lacewing and hoverfly larvae. Sap is hardly a balanced diet and in order to obtain enough non-carbohydrate nutrients, including protein, aphids take in an excess of

Figure 7.2 Ant 'milking' an aphid

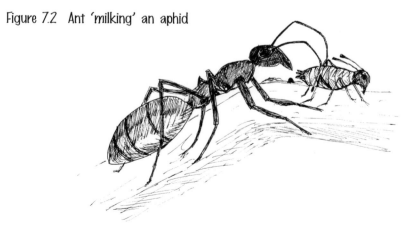

carbohydrates: this they excrete as sugary droplets, which are much to the taste of ants. These may be seen eliciting secretion by touching the aphids with their antennae – sometimes referred to as 'milking' (see Figure 7.2). Thus ants appear to herd these 'cattle' and to protect them from other insects. This relationship can hardly be regarded as permanent but will last as long as aphids are about and, in some cases, subterranean ants maintain 'herds' of aphids more or less continuously.

Rotten logs

Not all gardens have rotten logs, and even where they are potentially available they tend to be tidied away. Where they occur, however, they generally harbour a community of animals, within the wood, under the bark or under the log itself. This is because the log offers small creatures protection from birds, mice and toads, for example, but not from other small creatures, such as predatory ground beetles and centipedes.

Centipedes (which commonly have about 20 pairs of legs – one pair per segment, whereas millipedes have two) breed under logs and feed on the woodlice and other invertebrates that feed on the rotting wood. Millipedes, which are not carnivorous, are also found and are presumably too well armoured to be attacked by other small creatures. Earthworms often surface from burrows under the log and slugs commonly lay their pearly-white/yellowish eggs there.

Another of the reasons for these creatures coming together is that the log offers protection from drying out: the underside of logs tends to be very humid, especially if the log is large. The rain falling on the whole log probably trickles down to the smaller area in contact with the ground. This is very important for slugs but much less so for the chitin-encased beetles that may feed on them.

A selection of the creatures commonly found under a log is illustrated in Figure 7.3. Since there is little light there is, of course, hardly any plant life, but small fungi are found.

Flower beds

These are deliberately contrived communities, chosen because they flourish under similar conditions of soil texture, pH and water-holding capacity, and of aspect and thus exposure to sunlight. They

Figure 7.3 Animals found under logs

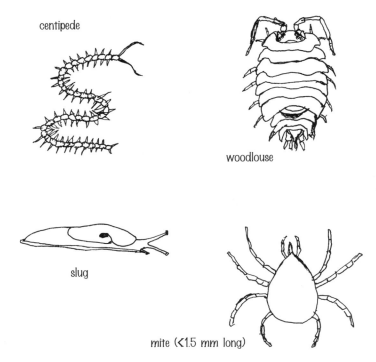

centipede

woodlouse

slug

mite (<1.5 mm long)

are also at least compatible with, if not complementary to, each other. They may combine plants of different heights, as in natural communities (such as beechwoods with bluebells), but they are unlikely to be interspersed, being designed to be seen, with taller species usually placed at the back of the bed. However, as in natural ecosystems, different species may grow and flower at different times of the year. They may not be limited to flowering plants and may contain annuals, perennials, shrubs and even creepers.

The emphasis is on plants, not animals, although some species (for example *Buddleja* spp.) are deliberately planted to attract the butterflies that feed on them. The plants that they lay their eggs on are rarely planted, though nettles may be preserved in odd corners for red admirals to breed on. Flowers may also be grown to attract beneficial insects. For example, one American ornamental garden plant, *Phacelia*, is very attractive to hover-flies (flower flies), whose larvae are major predators on aphids.

Flower beds are mainly designed for appearance, of flowers and foliage, but sometimes species are selected for their scent. Very often, heavily scented flowers smell strongest after dark, perhaps to attract pollinating moths.

Colonies

Some of the most evident social groupings are colonies of the same species. Such groupings may form for a variety of reasons. Social insects, such as ants, bees and wasps, form colonies because they operate this way, often with specialized functions (for example queens, drones, workers, soldiers), but even solitary bees and wasps may nest in closely adjacent groups.

Colonies tend to be formed by species whose members range quite widely, so that the concentration of individuals does not lead to competition for food. In the case of social insects, of course, the individuals behave co-operatively anyway. Bats and starlings, each sharing a common roost for the individuals of their species, and rooks nesting in colonies, all range widely for their food.

It is not obvious why rooks nest in colonies and crows do not. Rooks' nests (and the rooks) are very noticeable and crows much less so. It seems likely that a rookery offers protection from egg-stealers, such as jays, magpies and squirrels and it may be that crows need a much larger area to support them (on carrion) than is needed for rooks (feeding on soil invertebrates such as leatherjackets).

Crows' nests are typically placed high up in a single-stemmed tree (see Figure 7.4) but they also nest in tall but bushy conifers (pines, cedars). Indeed, in the past, so familiar was the crow's nest to countrymen that sailors christened the look-out position at the top of the main mast 'the crow's nest'. Although the illustration shows the *Mary Rose* (a 16th-century British galleon), the term was still in use until radar displaced look-outs. Indeed, in the Second World War, when I served in the Royal Navy, I spent many hours up the mast in a frigate's 'crow's nest'.

Figure 7.4 Typical position of a crow's nest

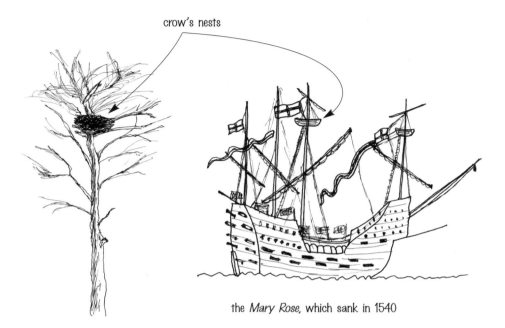

crow's nests

the *Mary Rose,* which sank in 1540

In plants, there is no real equivalent to the animal colony, except perhaps in simple aquatic forms (for example blanket weed in ponds).

Symbiosis

Symbiosis is a mutually beneficial (usually close) relationship between two different organisms. Good examples in plants are lichens (Box 7.3) and legumes with nitrogen-fixing bacteria in the roots (Box 7.4).

Plant/animal interactions

There are many interactions that fall short of the special cases described above. All animals that eat plants (herbivores) obviously have effects on the plants they consume, often destroying them completely. Rabbits are primarily grazing animals but they also

Box 7.3 Lichens

These are a large and successful group of plants, usually found on trees, gates, walls, paths or other flattish surfaces. Each plant consists of a fungus, which forms the outer layer, and algal cells entangled in fungal threads in the inner layer.

Buellia canescens is common on the bark of trees and on rocks and walls, forming closely attached patches, bluish grey (pale green when wet), lobed at the margins and often with white, powdery reproductive structures (soredia) at the centre. However, the variety of size, form and colour is very great between species: some are attached at a point but others are attached over the whole of the lower surface and thus cannot be removed without tearing.

Box 7.4 Nodules of legumes

The legumes (for example clover, vetches, lupins, alfalfa, peas and beans) are able to fix atmospheric nitrogen and thus be independent of the nitrates available in the soil. Sometimes this helps them in a drought, as can be seen in lawns where clover patches remain green when grasses fail to thrive: both may get water from depth but the soil nitrogen needed by the grass tends to be nearer the surface where the roots find themselves dried out.

This ability to fix atmospheric nitrogen is due to the presence of bacteria (the species varies with the species of plant but the genus *Rhizobium* is found in clovers, peas and beans) in nodules on the roots. These bacteria are able to fix nitrogen and release it directly to the plant (for example for protein formation) or, on the death of the root, to the soil. Some non-leguminous plants (for example the alder tree and the aquatic fern *Azolla*) are also able to do this, using bacteria, and there are free-living bacteria in the soil that have the same ability (for example the genus *Azotobacter*).

nodules

Nodules on roots of red clover

browse and it is the latter habit that is so destructive when directed at garden plants. They will nip off seedlings, including those of trees, and gnaw at the bark of somewhat larger trees and bushes, causing considerable damage.

Figure 7.5 The structure of grasses

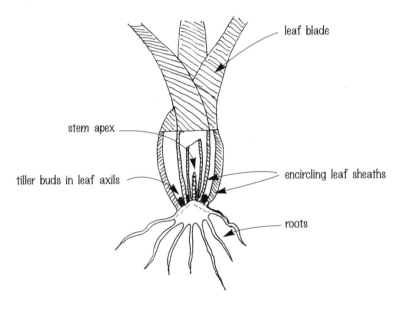

However, genuine grazing, of grass, does no harm at all. This is because the growing tip, or meristem, of grasses is very close to the ground (see Figure 7.5), so grazing (or cutting as in lawnmowing) the leaves does not damage the growing point. Regrowth occurs from this point but, in addition, closely defoliated grass tends to send out branches or 'tillers,' thus making the lawn more dense. That is why the creation of a dense lawn depends upon frequent close cutting. When rabbits were common on British downland, a short, fine grass cover resulted from their grazing.

Other herbivores behave differently, although wood-pigeons will often remove quite a lot of grass – and especially clover leaf. The commonest leaf eaters in gardens are caterpillars of butterflies and moths and include a great variety of forms, colours and species. In spite of their numbers they are not easily seen, due to their protective coloration and their habit of hiding under the leaf. The damage to the leaf is obvious, however, and, although unsightly, is often tolerated by the plant.

Plant leaves also suffer damage due to mining and tunnelling by larvae, for example those of the tomato leafminer, *Liriomyza bryonaie*, a small black fly 2.5 mm (about 1/8 in) long, which feeds on sap exuding from punctures on the leaf surface, made by females looking for egg-laying sites. The formation of galls around parasite larvae is another cause of damage (see Box 7.5).

Box 7.5 Galls and their formation

As illustrated below, galls may be noticeable, even spectacular, but the enormous variety of galls includes many, smaller, much less evident examples.

Galls on oak trees

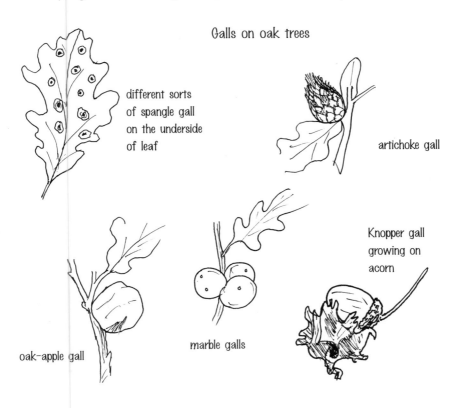

different sorts of spangle gall on the underside of leaf

artichoke gall

Knopper gall growing on acorn

oak-apple gall

marble galls

Galls are generally the result of a plant's reaction to the presence of an egg or a developing larva in its tissues, which proliferate to isolate the intruder, usually in a form that is almost external to the plant. Most galls are caused by insects (see Table 7.5), but in the UK about 50 different galls are caused by mites, while others are due to fungi or even eelworms. The greatest number of galls seem to occur on trees, especially oaks, sallows and willows – but not chestnuts. The bunches of twigs often seen on birches and called 'witches' brooms' are galls caused by mites, as are the 'nail galls' on lime leaves and 'big-bud' in blackcurrants.

In addition to the gall-former, several other species, including parasites of the gall-former, also live within the gall. These uninvited guests are called inquilines and form quite distinct and self-contained communities.

Table 7.5 Examples of galls caused by insects

Insect group	Species	Plant species	Nature of gall
Hymenoptera Gall-wasps and saw-flies	*Rhodites rosae* (a gall wasp)	Rose	Bedeguar
	Aulax glechomae (a gall wasp)	Ground ivy	Pea-sized, reddish, on stems and leaves
	Pontania proxima (a saw-fly)	Willows	Bean-shaped projection from both sides of the leaf
Diptera Gall-midges	*Perrisia ulmariae*	Meadowsweet	Numerous (30–200) reddish pustules on upper leaf surface with later some underneath
Hemiptera Aphids	*Capitophorus ribis*	White and red currants	Red, blister-like patches on underside of leaves

Among the most damaging leaf-eaters are slugs and snails. These emerge mainly at night and require damp conditions: they retire to hiding places during the day, under stones, in hedgerows, under bark or underground. Snail consumption by thrushes is well known: less well known are the predators of slugs, including frogs and toads but also predatory beetles (see Box 7.6).

Box 7.6 Predatory beetles

Ground-beetles (family *Carabidae*) are very agile and catch their prey, usually soil-dwelling creatures, using their powerful mandibles. Of more than 700 species in the UK, several occur in most gardens but they need stones or logs to hide under during the day: they are undoubtedly friends of the gardener.

The tiger-beetles (family *Cicindelidae*) are often more brightly coloured (for example green with red spots in *Cicindela campestris* but they tend to occur on sandy heaths and moorlands). Ladybirds (family *Coccinelidae*) have been referred to in the text: they do not need to be very active!

In ponds, there are large carnivorous water-beetles (family *Dytiscidae*). Beetle larvae are also carnivorous and thus may help to control pests.

Adult beetles are often quite large (for example 2 cm/^{3}/$_4$ in long) and have hard wing cases. In the rove beetles (family *Staphylinidae*) these wing cases only extend part of the way back, leaving the abdomen exposed. All are predacious and beneficial in both adult and larval phases.

Ground beetle
(length 26 mm/1 in)

Plants are not without defences, of course, ranging from hairs, thick waxy cuticles and poisonous or sticky sap to the presence of poisons within the leaf tissues. However, insects – especially sap-suckers – may act as vectors for virus or fungal diseases of plants (as with the elm bark beetle already mentioned). For every animal species that feeds on a plant, there are usually several species that feed on it, either by predation or by parasitism.

Animals and plants also interact by virtue of seed-eating or seed collection, chiefly by birds.

All this occurs above ground but, less obviously, there are also animals feeding on the roots (see Box 7.7).

Box 7.7 Root feeders

Many small animals feed on the roots of plants: the range is illustrated here with two examples.

Leatherjackets

These are the larvae of the crane-fly (*Tipula oleracea*) or 'daddy-longlegs'. The adults are particularly noticeable in late summer and early autumn, when the adults may emerge in numbers and mating occurs, especially in long grass. Each female may lay about 300 eggs and these hatch in about 14 days into larvae that feed on the roots, tubers and corms of plants, right through the autumn, winter and spring. The larvae grow to a length of 2–3 cm ($3/4$–$1 1/4$ in), are greyish-brown in colour, with a tough leathery skin, and can cause great damage to lawns, vegetables and flowers. Following such damage, other pests (for example millipedes) move in.

Looking at an insect simply as a pest is, of course, only one point of view (however understandable): clearly other crane-flies see things differently. Looking more closely at a crane-fly reveals some fascinating details. For example, the wings are large and obvious but there is only one pair. The hindmost pair have been modified to form 'halteres' or 'balancers', which are used in keeping the insect correctly oriented. Many flies have these

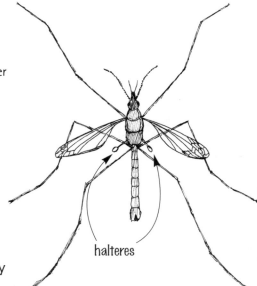

halteres

Crane fly

organs but they are usually much smaller and very difficult to spot. Crane-flies are about the best insects on which to see them: they are large, abundant, easily caught and easily held for examination.

Wireworms

Wireworms are larvae of the click beetle (*Agriotes* spp.) and are very widely distributed. The insect gets its name from its ability to curve its body and suddenly straighten out (with a clicking sound), jumping vertically in the air. The larvae live underground for four to five years, feeding on the underground parts of plants, before pupating. They have elongated bodies but only three pairs of legs at the front, whereas millipedes and centipedes have numerous pairs of legs all the way along their bodies.

It is worth remembering that both leatherjackets and wireworms are the favoured foods of many birds, especially rooks, crows and starlings. In fact, the number of insectivorous birds (and many of our garden birds are insect eaters) is bound to depend upon the source of food. So, no pests – no birds!

Predation

Predators are animals that kill and eat others: only a few are cannibals, usually when overcrowding leads to excessive competition for food (as can occur with tadpoles of the common frog).

Predators usually live on a number of other species, although one species may predominate. Foxes, for example, are commonly thought of as predators on rabbits, mice, voles but they also eat frogs, beetles and birds' eggs: some foxes have been found to feed, at times, mainly on earthworms.

The main garden predators are listed in Table 7.1 and, since gardens are usually cultivated for their plants, all these predators are essentially useful. The number of individual predators is usually low per unit area of land. Clearly, they have to be less numerous than the animals they live on, but by a surprisingly large margin since the prey population has to be able to reproduce and maintain its numbers or it will cease to exist. Consequently, the area required to support a fox that only ate rabbits would be much larger than that needed by a rabbit – probably a hundred times as great.

Table 7.1 Garden predators

Predator	Prey
Mammals	
Fox	Rabbits, voles, earthworms, beetles
Shrew	Earthworms, snails, insects
Squirrels	Nestlings
Hedgehogs	Slugs
Bats	Flying insects
Birds	
Owl	Voles, mice
Woodpeckers	Spotted: tree insects; Green: ants
Magpies and jays	Eggs, nestlings
All insectivorous birds, e.g.	
Blackbird	Insects, earthworms, caterpillars
Thrush	especially snails
Robin	Insects, earthworms
Tits	Especially aphids and caterpillars
Warblers	Insects
Reptiles	
Grass snake	Frogs, newts, mice, voles
Fish	
Most common species	Aquatic insects and mosquito larvae
Amphibians	**All, when in water, insects**
Frog	Flies
Toad	Beetles, slugs
Newt	Water fleas and shrimps, aquatic insect larvae
Arachnids	
Spider	Insects
Harvestman	Insects
Insects	
Wasps	Insects to feed their grubs
Carabid beetles	Slugs
Ladybirds	Aphids
Hover-fly larvae	Aphids
Solitary wasps	Caterpillars, spiders, bees
Ants	Insects

It therefore makes sense for predators to eat a variety of other species and enjoy the flexibility that confers: after all, species vary in their availability at different times of the year (some even hibernate). It would therefore be difficult for a predator to live solely on another predator species, as the area needed to support it would be enormous. It is much more common for herbivorous species to specialize on one kind of plant and, very often, on only one part of it (for example leaf, root, pollen).

Predators, by the very nature of things, tend to be bigger than their prey, unless the predatory individuals are very fierce or cooperate in packs. In the garden, probably only ants come into this last category, often combining to kill a beetle much larger than themselves.

Parasites, however, have to be smaller than their hosts and, in general, they are very small indeed – but may still be numerous.

Parasitism

Virtually every species of plant and animal found in a garden – as elsewhere – will have one or more parasites, though this may not be true of every individual, of course. Parasites live on (external parasites) or in (internal) their host and, in most cases, do not result in its death, unless at a time that allows the survival of the parasites. Those that do kill the host are often called parasitoids.

So widespread is parasitism that it has been said that if all organisms disappeared except parasitic nematodes (roundworms, such as occur in puppies), the living world would still be represented by a ghostly shadow of itself in the form of these parasites.

The extraordinary variety of forms and life-cycles, some of them sounding almost beyond belief, can hardly even be indicated here: a few common examples will have to serve.

External parasites of animals
Mites of the genus *Parasitus* are found in large numbers on bumble-bees and in their nests. When queen bumble-bees emerge from winter hibernation and are foraging in mid-spring or searching for a nest-site, seething masses of these brown eight-legged mites may be observed clinging to their bodies, chiefly on the thorax and abdomen.

However, they may live mainly on scraps of pollen and even keep the comb and bodies of the bees clean – they may do no harm at all. Animals which live together in this way are called commensals and commensalism is really a form of close association.

Conversely, an external parasite of honey-bees is currently causing severe problems: this is the varroa mite (see Box 7.8).

Box 7.8 Varroa mites

Along with spiders, mites belong to the order *Arachnida*, all of which have eight legs. There are many pestiferous mites (for example the fruit tree red spider mite) and useful ones (for example *Typhlodromus pyri* – see Box 7.9) that prey on them. There are also harmless mites, such as those on bumble-bees (see below), but the varroa mite (*Varroa facolsoni*) is a major disaster for honey-bees. It arrived in the UK in 1991 from mainland Europe and is now a huge problem for honey producers. The adult females feed on the blood of adult bees and on developing pupae but they can also transmit virus infections: the combined effect can wipe out whole colonies.

Mites on bumble-bees

In addition to the apparently harmless *Parasitus* mites, other tiny mites (probably *Tarsonoemus* spp.) live in the abdominal air-sacs of bumble-bees, living on body-juices but apparently doing little harm. They overwinter on the hibernating queens and when the latter emerge in the spring they are often covered, especially on the thorax, with these small, brown, eight-legged creatures – quite easily visible to the naked eye. That is because they have emerged from the air-sacs to travel about on the outside of the queen in order to infect the workers, where a similar cycle occurs.

Nematodes in slugs

Nematodes are roundworms (*Nematoda*), commonly thread-like, that parasitize the bodies of animals, sometimes living in the gut but often penetrating other tissues. They are the roundworms of humans, dogs, cats, cattle, sheep and horses and there may be many thousands in the host's stomach and/or intestines. They lay eggs that are passed out in the faeces and after (usually two) larval stages enter the third or infective larval stages, in which, when the larvae are eaten by another individual, they become mature and start the whole process again. These gut worms may suck blood or feed on the gut wall – unlike tape-worms, which just lie in the intestinal 'soup' – but only kill if present in very large numbers. The species which kills slugs has only recently been identified (*Phasmarhabditis hermaphrodita*) and is now being used as a form of biological control (see later). There are also free-living nematodes, for example in the soil, and parasitic ones in plants – called 'eelworms'.

The rose gall (bedeguar)

This occurs mainly on wild roses but is also found on cultivated rambler roses that have been allowed to grow freely. It is a spectacular-looking, reddish gall (called the 'bedeguar gall', 'moss gall' or 'robin's pincushion') and is caused by a tiny gall-wasp (*Rhodites rosae*). The gall may be over 2.5 cm (1 in) across and is best seen in mid to late summer. It contains several cells, each with a single *Rhodites* larva living on the tissue grown by the plant in response to the gall-wasp egg being laid. The gall-wasp also has parasites and several other species of insect may live in the gall.

Galls occur in a vast variety of forms on all kinds of plants and may be caused by saw-flies or true flies (*Dipterans*). Oak-apple galls (see Box 7.5) are a very common example, also caused by a gall-wasp (*Biorhiza pallida*) and, if the gall is cut open, the wasp grub will be found inside. Oak-leaves, in about midsummer, bear circular growths on the underside of the leaf; these are called 'common spangle' galls and are also caused by gall-wasps.

Plant parasites

Plant parasites are relatively uncommon except for fungi. Mistletoe is considered as a half-parasite, because it contains chlorophyll and thus carries out its own photosynthesis. Broomrapes (*Orobanche* spp.) have no chlorophyll and the mature dodder (*Cuscata* spp.) is also entirely dependent on its host plant for water and all its nutrients.

Fleas

Some animal parasites, on the other hand, appear to be almost ubiquitous. Fleas are well known, especially on cats, but they occur on many furry animals, including moles and rabbits, and are well adapted to birds. Their vertically flattened bodies allow them to slip easily between hairs or feathers.

Fleas suck blood but can survive for substantial periods away from the host. The larvae and pupae are not to be found on the animal but in its nest (or burrow), where the larvae feed on organic debris.

Fleas are adapted to their hosts and their life-cycles fit the hosts' habits. Thus, bird fleas are most active during nesting and presumably thrive better in those birds, such as house martins, that return to the same nests. There may be many reasons why most birds build new nests each year, but the avoidance of parasites may be one of them. Certainly, fleas thrive in house martins' nests. Miriam Rothschild, in her famous book *Fleas, Flukes and Cuckoos* (Collins, 1952), gave the maximum number of fleas recovered from a house martin as 25, but 4,000 were bred from a single nest!

Any animal that feeds on another species may have some effect on the numbers of that species. This regulation of the numbers of one species by another is called biological control but, before considering that, it is helpful to appreciate the enormous potential for reproduction possessed by many organisms.

Reproductive potential

It follows from the numbers of seeds that plants can produce (see Table 1.1) that if they all survived to produce new plants we would be submerged very quickly. But since this is true for each species, it is clear that it cannot happen and that there are controls, imposed by competition, disease, destruction by animals and so on.

Fortunately, the same is true for animals. A long time ago, it was calculated that the common housefly could produce 120 eggs per female and seven generations per year. Half the offspring would be females and, with no controls, there would be an astounding 5,700 billions at the end of the year, all derived from the one original fly.

It may be thought that such numbers could only apply to very small organisms, and there is some truth in this. However, Charles Darwin calculated that one pair of elephants would generate 19 million descendants after 750 years!

An intermediate example is that of the house sparrow. When it was first introduced into the United States, it was estimated that, in ten years, one pair would produce 275,716,698 descendants. Of course, this did not happen and less than 5 per cent of these numbers materialized.

These calculations illustrate the need for the kind of interactions described earlier. The resulting interacting pattern of species and numbers is referred to as the 'balance of nature'. It is the result of many adjustments to the reproductive rate to keep it in line with such losses and with food supply.

Biological control

There are two distinct definitions of the term biological control: (1) The deliberate use of one species to control another with the aim of utilizing natural enemies to reduce the damage caused by noxious organisms to tolerable levels; and (2) One of the major ecological forces of nature, the regulation of plant and animal members by natural enemies.

The first definition describes the applied activity on farms and in gardens to introduce, protect or culture enemies of those organisms that are seen as undesirable (weeds or pests), in order to redress an unwanted balance. The latter has often arisen because of the artificial concentration of plants and animals that occurs both on farms and in gardens. We are not satisfied with sharing our products or our plants with a host of other species that consume them or spoil their appearance, so, in a desire to maintain an essentially unnatural balance, favouring our chosen species at the expense of their pests or competitors, we seek to deploy their enemies in a controlled manner.

Pesticides and herbicides are the alternative control measures but these are sometimes rather indiscriminate in their effect and their residues may accumulate in the food chain. In an effort to minimize chemical usage, therefore, both on farms and in gardens, biological control is being used, alone or in conjunction with chemicals (the so-called 'integrated pest management' concept). The fact is, however, that the second definition always applies as well, unless the natural forces are distorted, by chemicals, cultural regimes or management.

All kinds of organism can be used, including the nematodes that parasitize slugs, mentioned earlier in this chapter. Three contrasting examples are described here: (1) ladybirds and aphids; (2) mites on apple and pear trees; and (3) nematodes and slugs.

Ladybirds and aphids

There are some 42 species of ladybirds (family *Coccinellidae*) in the UK of which about 24 are commonly found, the most common being the two-spot (*Adalia bipunctata*) and the seven-spot (*Coccinella 7-punctata*), though even within a species there is much colour variation. They lay small yellow eggs on the undersides of leaves infested with aphids and both adults and larvae are carnivorous, often virtually confining themselves to a diet of greenfly. A typical life-cycle is shown below.

Figure 7.6 Life cycle of a 7-spot ladybird

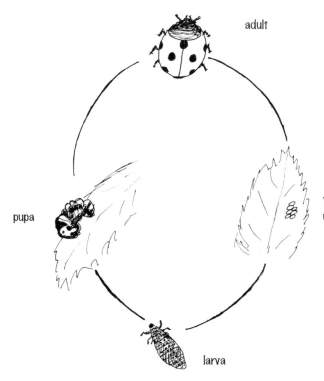

adult

yellow eggs on
underside of leaf

pupa

larva

Their bright colours are examples of warning coloration (as with wasps), alerting potential predators to the fact that they are unpleasant in taste: indeed, when attacked, they ooze drops of caustic blood from their joints. Another example of this method of deterrence is the magpie moth, whose colourful caterpillars feed on gooseberry and currant bushes.

The two-spot ladybird is often most noticeable when it hibernates, since dozens may be found together under bark, in cupressus hedges and in houses, where they are most obvious in early spring on window ledges, having emerged from the cracks where they have overwintered.

Ladybirds can be collected and deliberately placed on plants infested with aphids as a form of biological control. Other species also eat aphids. For example, hover-flies eat 50–60 aphids a day but they also need pollen, so planting a good source of it, such as *Phacelia*, serves to attract them and can have a marked effect on aphid numbers.

Mites on apple and pear trees

Among the most important pests on apple trees are the fruit tree red spider mite (*Panonychus ulmi*) and the apple rust mite (*Aculus schlechtendali*). Both are attacked by yet another mite (*Typhlodromus pyri*); these are often referred to as 'typhs'. Box 7.9 describes how these are used in biological control.

Nematodes and slugs

Slugs, of which there are about six species in British gardens (see Box 7.10), are notoriously damaging and difficult to control, so the recent discovery that the nematode *Phasmarhabditis hermaphrodita* can be used as a biological control agent is of great interest to gardeners. In 1993, it was found that the 1 mm-long nematodes appeared to infest and kill slugs but it transpired that they achieve this by introducing bacteria. Mixtures of worms and bacteria can now be applied with a watering can: they only target slugs and snails, so no damage is done to beneficial organisms such as earthworms.

Ducks have also been used to control slugs and obviously many bird species might eat the infected slugs. However, since the nematodes die at normal body temperatures, it is thought that wild fauna and birds would be unaffected. Awareness of such sequential effects is

---

Box 7.9 The use of typhs

Apple trees have many pests (many more than pears, for example), one of them being the very small apple rust mite, *Aculus schlechtendali*, which overwinters in sheltered crevices on the tree and feeds on the undersides of the leaves. Although populations of several hundred mites per leaf may not appear to cause much damage, they can also feed on the developing fruitlets and cause 'russeting' of the apple surface. A second mite, the fruit tree red spider mite (*Panonychus ulmi*) also feeds on the undersides of leaves, with similar effects on the leaves, but does not damage the fruit.

Yet another mite, *Typhlodromus pyri*, is a major predator of both of these pests and often builds up its numbers on selectively sprayed orchards. This is because it has become resistant to several major pesticides, including OPs (organophosphates), so that these can be used to control other pest species without damaging the typhs. Integrated pest management (IPM) is based on this ability to combine biological control with the selected use of chemicals.

---

extremely important when trying to manipulate natural populations.

Quite a few of the larger carabid beetles (especially *Pterostichus melanarius*) may be important predators but they clearly do not offer enough control, since the problems are commonplace and there may be as many as 200 slugs to every 1 m^2 (11 sq ft) of soil.

Conservation

Living things cannot, of course, be preserved beyond their normal life-span and, for most organisms, this is relatively short, partly because there is a longevity limit but mostly because most animals and plants do not enjoy the luxury of old age or medical treatment. Most are killed by predation, parasitism, disease, accident or starvation. Trees are rather exceptional: very small organisms' lives are measured in hours, days or weeks and even most garden birds last for only a few years.

Conservation therefore usually has to mean of the species or the habitat that supports it: indeed, it is hard to conserve the former without the latter. Gardens are not usually designed for any such

Box 7.10 Slugs

Slugs are molluscs and there are several species that are commonly found in gardens.

Common name	Latin name	Colours	Size (mm)	Eggs
Field slug	*Agriolimax reticulatus*	Fawn/light brown	20–25	Spherical and translucent
Garden slug	*Arion hortensis*	Black with yellow foot	25–30	Spherical and opaque
White-soled dark slug	*Arion fasciatus*	Greyish black above with dark lateral strands. Foot white	30–35	Yellow or amber
Black slug	*Arion ater*	Black with paler underside	200	Opaque and leathery
Great slug	*Limax maximum*	Greyish-brown with spotted mantle	100–200	Amber and translucent
Keeled slug	*Limax budapestensis*	Brown or black with light keel or ridge down the back	50	Translucent

Several species are major pests of brassicas, particularly the small grey field slug and especially the juveniles.

It might be thought that grass could hardly be affected, and it is true that other plants are preferred, but if for example the grass *Poa annua* is attacked, slugs may actually kill the plant by eating out the meristem. Slugs have a quite disproportionate effect on seedlings, of course. All slugs require moisture – at all stages, including the egg – and hide away during the day and dry periods, in cracks in the soil and under stones, logs, and so forth.

---

purpose but can be modified to do so and, in any event, they represent a habitat of their own and include any number of minor habitats within them.

Modifications

The inclusion of a pond can help to conserve amphibians, shrubbery may provide nest sites for birds, wilder patches may offer breeding and feeding sites for butterflies and moths, seed heads left in place provide food for birds and weevils, rough grass offers cover for voles, ants and shrews, hedgerows accommodate field mice, bumble-bees and nesting birds, and unsprayed brickwork may provide sites for solitary bees and wasps. Old fence posts may be peppered with small holes of the powder post beetles (*Lyctus* spp.) and these may subsequently be used by small solitary wasps.

Rotting logs will often contain the larvae of a variety of beetles (for example the wasp-beetle, with somewhat the colouring of a wasp) including one of our largest and most spectacular, the stag beetle, *Lucanas cervus* (see Figure 7.7). Now a protected species in the UK (protected by law from destruction or even interference, though foxes appear not to have heard of this), the stag beetle lays its eggs on rotting logs and the larvae burrow about deep inside for up to four (or even, in some species, six) years, eventually pupating in the log. These larvae are large, whitish and fleshy, with a hard brown head and six legs just behind it. Simply leaving a few such logs about, instead of tidying them away or burning them, can contribute to the conservation of what is now considered to be a rare species.

Figure 7.7   Stag beetle

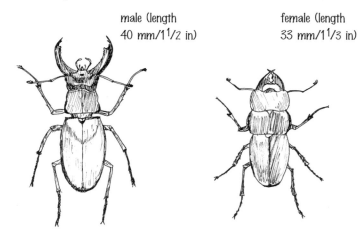

male (length
40 mm/1 1/2 in)

female (length
33 mm/1 1/3 in)

Aids to observation

All these sites may greatly increase the chance of seeing small creatures but how much you can see depends also on whether you use any aids (for example binoculars or a magnifying glass). Magnifying things may seem a bit technical, but most of us would not leave our glasses behind when we go out in to the garden! Just as sunglasses may help you to see in bright sunshine, so night-vision glasses can help in the dark.

Devices may be used to create sites, such as covers under which small creatures gather. Dustbin lids are one example, but corrugated iron sheets have been used for snakes to hide under. Very often it is useful to mark a place, where a bumble-bee is seen to enter a hole in the ground, for example. Golf tees are useful for this.

Observations can often be more interesting if they are recorded in a diary. It is also useful to measure things, for example employing a rain gauge to measure rainfall or a maximum/minimum thermometer. A sundial is a way of measuring time but also, directly, of where the sun is at certain times.

You can make yourself less conspicuous (avoid bright clothes and wear camouflage!) in order to avoid frightening animals, and you can draw/map what you see. There is nothing like drawing an animal or a plant to make sure that you observe every detail.

8 Control in the Garden

It is not difficult to accept that control is necessary in a garden. The lawn is the simplest example. If you did not cut it, it would become longer and tussocky, more difficult to walk on, impossible to play croquet or clock-golf on, and, eventually, it would probably become scrub leading to woodland or forest as tree and shrub seedlings grew unchecked. Unless, that is, it was closely grazed by, for example, rabbits. A lawn is, by definition, a controlled area of grass and grasses respond to regular and frequent defoliation by tillering (branching) and producing a dense mat of leaves (see Chapter 3).

Other plants, such as roses, have to be controlled by pruning, either to create and retain the desired shape or to stimulate flower production. Creating shape is seen in its most extreme form in topiary but this does not usually involve very frequent clipping, since the shrubs involved are usually fairly slow-growing. In fact, the majority of pruning is not much more than annual, although privet hedges require more frequent cutting than that. Yew hedges develop incredibly dense, packed growth, even under an annual clipping regime.

All this is very familiar to the gardener, as are dead-heading, removal of dead wood or vegetation, and the pinching out of young, unwanted shoots. These activities are aimed at controlling the growth of the cultivated plants: weeding is aimed at removing the unwanted species. What is regarded as a weed leaves room for some argument, especially in regard to the lawn. Some gardeners want to retain only the finest of fine-leaved grasses while others accept some clover, daisies and a variety of small-leaved herbs. Moss is generally frowned on, although it makes a wonderfully soft surface for walking on, and some lawns are actually made of non-grass species (for example chamomile *Anthemis nobilis* or *Matricaria chamomilla*) in order to reduce or eliminate altogether the need for cutting.

Weeding, of course, like sowing and planting, is designed to favour particular species, and, indeed, varieties, that are preferred.

Sometimes this has to do with producing sequences of colour or patterns, involving not just colour but also height and density, to create the most attractive appearance. In such schemes, even non-weeds, desired in another part of the garden, are removed or, sometimes, moved. Although these primary objectives have to take precedence, it is often worth considering the consequences in terms, for example, of what kind of birds or butterflies will be attracted. As pointed out elsewhere, seed-eating birds, such as the goldfinch, may only appear in gardens with plentiful seed heads and butterflies have marked preferences (see Chapter 4).

Mechanical operations such as those described, are, of course, not the only ways to control vegetation growth. Watering and fertilizing exert very marked effects on growth but not all species require, or can even tolerate, high levels of either.

In addition to physical methods, a variety of chemicals are available, especially for the control of weeds. Again, it is worth considering the incidental effects of chemical use. However, there are some weeds (for example stinging nettle, ground elder and couch grass) that are extremely difficult to get rid of mechanically: they seem to regrow from tiny pieces of root or stem.

Herbicides and hormones

These substances are artificial aids to control in the garden and many are very effective. Organic gardeners choose to avoid them and prefer to depend upon 'natural' processes, though it has to be admitted that there are difficulties in arguing that gardening itself is 'natural' or does not interfere with nature. But, then, 'nature' interferes with 'nature', in the sense that species compete and, as described in Chapter 7, the 'balance of nature' depends upon animals eating plants and other animals, as well as plants competing with each other for light, space and nutrients. Gardening is an attempt to modify this balance so that our own activities and preferences dominate the result. Chemicals are not so different from other weapons and, indeed, plants and animals use them too (see Table 8.1). Some of the most virulent poisons are perfectly natural.

Hormones also occur naturally and, indeed, both plants and

Table 8.1 Natural chemical weapons

Organism	Chemical weapon
Adder	Poison injected by biting (via hollow teeth)
Toad	Skin secretion of two poisons, bufotalin and bufogin (with an action akin to that of digitalis)
Bee	Sting injects several toxins, chiefly 'apitoxin'
Wasp	Sting injects amines and peptides (and neurotoxins)
Spanish fly (*Lytta vesicatoria*) (a green beetle)	Contains a blistering agent, cartharidin
Red ant (*Formica rufa*)	Discharges formic acid (up to 30 cm/12 in) from its tail end
Yew tree (*Taxus baccata*)	Taxol* in the bark halts cell division in pests
Bracken (*Pteridium aquilinum*)	Carcinogen in spores and poisonous to cattle, sheep and horses

* now the basis of an anti-cancer drug

animals depend upon them as 'messengers' to produce or stimulate essential responses. Few gardeners seem to worry about the use of hormones to stimulate rooting in cuttings: a very different reaction to that commonly found in relation to the use of hormones in farm livestock, for example.

One perfectly reasonable justification for reluctance to use 'artificial' herbicides is that we may not fully understand all the consequences of our actions, since the applied herbicide may have other effects than those for which they are used. (Mind you, life would be very difficult if we avoided any action where we could not foresee all the consequences!) The usual solution to this problem is to use herbicides (a) that can be placed exactly where they are wanted (that is, on the particular plant or even part of a plant) and (b) that are inactivated as soon as they reach the soil.

This is much more difficult to arrive at in the use of chemicals for pest control. Pesticides are chemicals that are toxic to pest organisms or, in some cases, disrupt their metabolic processes (such as interfering with essential moulting). More generally, we can refer to 'biocides', to include chemicals aimed at disease-producing organisms, especially fungi. The problem here is that their application cannot be confined to the target organism and may have to be used in considerable quantity in order to reach all the pests. It may therefore kill other organisms, many of which may be beneficial, so there may be unfortunate consequences, some unpredictable and some never known about. Moderate use may even allow the development of resistant strains of the pest and another chemical then has to be sought. Consequently, there are many reasons for considering some form of biological control (see also Chapter 7).

Biological control

The previous chapter pointed out that biological control goes on all the time, in addition to the efforts that we may make to modify the balance of predators, parasites and prey in our preferred direction. This will rarely provide adequate control, however, since both predators and parasites depend upon their prey for food. The prey species therefore have to survive in adequate numbers and the more predators there are, the more prey there have to be. So it is quite impossible to use predators to eliminate pests or even to keep them at a very low level, unless they only form a part of the predators' diet.

Usually, most pest species can breed faster than predators – that's why they are pests. Furthermore, the pest species have to start multiplying earlier, otherwise the increasing numbers of predators could not be fed. Figure 8.1 illustrates this 'lag' effect for predator/prey relationships.

Chapter 7 gave three examples of biological control that are actually manipulated in gardens and orchards: ladybirds on aphids, mites controlling other mites and nematodes controlling slugs. The last is an example where the controlling organism can actually breed faster than the prey: this is related to the fact that the former is much smaller than the latter.

Figure 8.1 Number of predators (broken line) and prey (continuous line), plotted against time as the horizontal axis

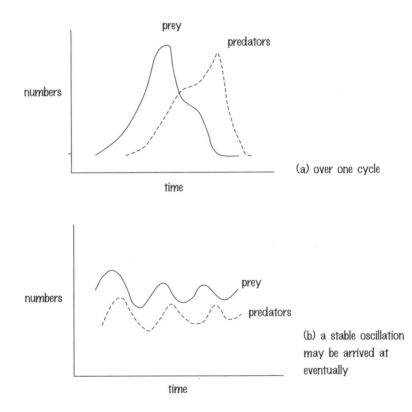

(a) over one cycle

(b) a stable oscillation may be arrived at eventually

It has to be remembered that these examples are oversimplified relationships. Commonly, more than one species of predator will feed on a prey species, but there will be others that eat the predators. Take the ladybird/aphid example – one of the best-known to gardeners. There are some 24 reasonably common species of ladybirds in Britain, varying greatly in size and coloration. The number of spots varies from the common two-spot (*Adalia bipunctata*), which is most usually red with black spots but may also occur with red spots on a black background, to the lemon-coloured 22-spot (*Thea 22-punctata*). All these are members of the family *Coccinellidae* (which has 5,200 species

Box 8.1 Reproduction in ladybirds

The small, yellow eggs are laid in groups (see Figure 7.4), usually on aphid-infested plants, often on the undersides of the leaves. These hatch to produce slate-blue larvae, often spotted and with many tubercles, tapering towards the posterior end and with well-developed legs. These larvae live for about three weeks, during which time they can devour several hundred aphids (in its lifetime a ladybird may consume 5500 aphids). They then pupate, usually attached to the underside of a leaf, and remain thus for about two weeks.

The seven-spot ladybird may be prevented from breeding by a parasitic wasp (*Dinocampus coccinellae*), which lays a single egg inside it. The resulting larva feeds on internal fat reserves and, later, the gonads, all without killing its host. When the larva is fully fed it severs the main nerves to the ladybird's legs, thus immobilizing it, and emerges through the abdomen to pupate underneath it. The ladybird continues to live, putting off predators by its warning coloration and exuding caustic blood from its joints if attacked. The wasp emerges before the ladybird dies of starvation and goes off to repeat the cycle (they are all females and do not need to mate).

---

worldwide). However, they all have similar life-histories (see Figure 7.4 and Box 8.1).

Because their prey are sedentary and soft-bodied, neither the adult nor the larvae have to be particularly agile or particularly equipped to detect or catch them. As it happens, not much feeds on ladybirds because, as can be guessed from their bright 'warning' coloration, they appear to have an unpleasant taste to birds. However, ants may defend the aphids they milk (see Chapter 7) and other creatures also eat the aphids (including larvae of hover-flies and lacewings). These include many small birds but especially blue tits, which can be seen searching for them on all kinds of plants.

Now, although ladybirds cannot control aphids completely, because they may live on nothing else, the blue tits are quite different. They do not depend on aphids but can eat vast numbers at exactly the times when they are most numerous. Furthermore, they can travel further and quicker than ladybirds and even more so than their larvae.

When it comes to reproduction, aphids are almost in a class of their own (see Box 8.2). Control by biological means alone is often quite difficult (see Box 8.3) but it is also difficult to use a chemical spray that will have no effect on beneficial organisms. This is especially so with sap-sucking creatures such as aphids, since their food cannot be sprayed (their stylets penetrate quite deep into plant tissues). Only contact sprays are effective and this involves saturation of surfaces in order to hit a high proportion of them.

Clearly, biological control and the integration of it with chemical methods requires considerable knowledge of all the organisms involved, their food, their life-cycles, their methods of reproduction, where they are at what times of the year; in short, their natural history.

Box 8.2 Reproduction in aphids

Aphids reproduce viviparously, the eggs being retained within the body of the female until they hatch. Shortly after that they are born as living young. It is not difficult to observe this, since it is happening most of the spring and summer in any colony of aphids. Only in the autumn do they produce eggs.

In addition, most of the young are produced by parthenogenesis (that is, without mating) and all the progeny are female, thus accelerating the reproductive rate. (Parthenogenesis is quite common in insects: in honey-bees it results in males and drones, whereas queens and workers result from eggs that have been fertilized.)

There are some 450 kinds of aphid in the UK: in gardens they are most noticeable on roses, broad beans and apple trees, but they occur on most plants at some time. In about mid-autumn they produce males and females that mate and lay fertilized eggs (relatively large, black and thick-shelled) and it is these that overwinter to hatch early in the following spring, usually on a woody plant. The wingless females that hatch out produce living young and among these some have wings. These 'migrants' spread out to the plants that will sustain colonies for the rest of the spring and summer.

A single aphid can produce several daughters daily and these progeny start reproducing themselves some 8–10 days later – faster if the weather is warm; cold slows them down. Thus one bean aphid (*Aphid fabae*) may give rise to over 1300 individuals at the end of 14 days, if the mean temperature is about 22°C (71°F). The bean aphid winters on the spindle-tree or guelder rose (*Viburnum opulus*).

Box 8.3 Examples of biological control

Agent	Pest
Viruses	
Bacculoviruses	Larval stages of butterflies and moths
	Ants, bees, wasps, flies, gnats, midges
Bacteria	
Bacillus thuringiensis	Moths, beetles, flies
Nematodes	
Phasmarhabditis hermaphrodita	Slugs
Steinernema feltiae	Fly larvae
Insects	
Parasitic wasps	Aphids and whitefly

One way of reducing the impact of pests and diseases is to breed relatively resistant varieties. After all, the thing that the gardener is most in control of is the choice of plants and, for some plants, the breeding of a new variety can be very rapid, particularly in the case of annuals. Furthermore, modern technology now offers possibilities that simply were not available before.

Control of breeding

Conventional breeding proceeds by the selection of better or preferred individuals and then breeding from them. Particular crosses can be made from parents chosen for their particular qualities. So new colours, sizes and shapes can be produced and this is now the basis of massive commercial activity.

The same processes can be applied to frost resistance, resistance to drought, salt tolerance and, of course, resistance to pests and diseases. This is easier for garden plants than for food crops, since some of the properties that protect plants from pests, such as the presence of toxic chemicals, are undesirable in food. Many plants are poisonous, including some very common ones (see Box 8.4).

Curiously enough, some of these toxins (such as allyl isothiacyanate in broccoli and brussels sprouts) are now thought to be possible anticarcinogens and thus beneficial! In some cases, insects actually absorb these plant poisons and use them for their own defence. Some bizarre examples of this are given in Box 8.5.

Box 8.4 Poisonous plants

A surprising number of plants are poisonous, though not necessarily to all animals and sometimes only when eaten in large quantities. The poisons are mainly alkaloids or glycosides but some volatile oils and resinous substances may also cause toxic effects.

Sometimes these poisons are destroyed by heat, in drying or cooking, and sometimes small quantities are useful medicinally. Quite often only a part of the plant is poisonous: examples are given below (the complete list is much longer):

Plant spp.	Poisonous part of the plant
Shrubs	
Broom	Seeds
Mistletoe	Berries
Rhododendron	Leaves and flowers
Privet	Berries and possibly leaves
Trees	
Holly	Berries
Yew	Leaves and seeds
Laburnum	All, but especially bark and seeds
Oak	Leaves and acorns
Beech	Nuts
Herbs	
Buttercups	Sap
Lily of the valley	All parts
Celandine	Sap
Bluebell	Bulbs
St John's wort	Leaves and flowers
Rhubarb	Leaves
Ragwort	All parts
Yellow vetchling	All, especially seeds
Tomato	Stem and leaves

Plant spp.	Poisonous part of the plant
Lupins	All, especially seeds, except for sweet lupin
Daffodil	Bulbs
Yellow flag	Leaves and rhizomes
Hellebores	All parts
Marsh marigold	Sap
Aquilegia	Possibly all
Foxglove	All parts
Cuckoo Pint	All, especially berries
Tobacco	Leaves
Climbers	
Ivy	Leaves and berries
White bryony	Roots and berries
Black bryony	Roots and berries
Fungi	
Boletus	Not certain
Agaric	Not certain
Ink cap	Not certain
Horsetails	
Equisetum spp.	Probably all parts
Ferns	
Bracken	Especially the rhizome

Box 8.5 Use of plant toxins by insects

Insect	Plant toxin absorbed
Leaf beetle (*Melasoma populi*) glands secrete salicyl-aldehyde	Derived from the glucoside salicin in dwarf sallows (willow)
Grasshopper (*Poekilocercus bufonius*)	Cardenolides from the leaves of milkweed (*Ascelepias curassavica*)
Monarch butterfly (*Danaus plexippus*)	Cardenolides from the leaves of milkweed (*Ascelepias curassavica*)

Plants have a whole range of protective mechanisms (see Table 8.2) which can be exploited by breeders, and the modern techniques of molecular biology can further extend the process. Such technology is artificial – but then so is gardening – and can produce results that could not occur without such technology. So, although it can be argued that science can now produce quite quickly, and with greater precision, what plant breeders would take many years to achieve, there are some fundamental differences. It is now possible to identify a gene for, let us say, resistance to disease, to isolate it and place it within a plant of a quite different species.

Table 8.2 Protective mechanisms in plants

Protective features	Examples
External	
Thick waxy cuticle	Holly
Spines on leaf	Holly
Spines on stems	Hawthorn
Internal	
Poisonous tissue	See Box 8.4
Irritants in hairs	Stinging nettle
Irritants in sap	Sage

In principle, this may not seem any different from the breeders' achievements, over many years, in producing flowers that are larger and with brighter colours than anything ever found in nature. The mechanisms employed, however, are entirely different and laboratory based. Most people are much more concerned about this in relation to animals, partly because animal welfare raises ethical issues not associated with plants. No gardener feels any compunction about cutting back on the growth of plants, eliminating surplus individuals or discarding mistakes in the breeding programme, but there are worries about genetically altered plants, especially those engineered to be resistant to particular chemical sprays (so that applications can eliminate the weeds without harming the chosen species). There are concerns that such resistance might somehow transfer itself to weeds, that would then become uncontrollable.

These are, of course, practical rather than ethical concerns. The latter do emerge in the case of food plants and, most particularly, if the consumer is unable to tell which products have been subjected to genetic manipulation and which have not. This is currently an important issue in the UK with imported soya beans and maize, both major commodities that are internationally traded and are incorporated in an enormous range of food products.

Such genetic modification is not allowed in current organic standards (see Box 8.6) but these only have legal force for foodstuffs. Insofar as 'organic' gardening follows the same rules, therefore, genetically modified organisms (as defined in modern biotechnology: all breeding, of course, results in genetic modification!) should not be used.

Box 8.6 Organic food production

Strictly speaking, the law about the use of the word 'organic' only applies to food produced for sale. A European Regulation (No. EEC 2092/91) is now in force, in all EU countries, that makes it illegal to label any foodstuff 'organic' unless it is produced to laid-down standards. Every EU member state is obliged to establish a body to implement these standards, to register every producer and to ensure that such producers' enterprises are inspected regularly by independent inspectors.

In the UK, the designated body is UKROFS (UK Register of Organic Food Standards), established in 1987, to which all the organic sector bodies (Soil Association, Organic Farmers & Growers, Biodynamic Association, Scottish Organic Producers Association, Organic Food Federation) belong. Its functions are currently being reviewed. No food can be sold as 'organic' that does not conform to all these rules. None of this applies to home-grown food crops, however, and many people would loosely describe their gardening as 'organic' or 'based on organic principles' if no chemical sprays or inorganic fertilizer were used. This usually means applying only organic manures or composts.

However, a major reason why chemicals are not used by organic enthusiasts is that they wish to work with nature and to encourage all the beneficial organisms. A positive approach to this requires some knowledge of all the organisms involved; in other words, 'organic' gardening (or farming) depends upon a knowledge of the relevant natural history.

Soil fertility control

By contrast with these applications of modern technology, gardeners have always made some attempt to affect plant growth by controlling soil fertility. This includes the use of fertilizers, to add the major nutrients (nitrogen, phosphate and potassium), but also to alter the acidity of the soil (its pH), commonly by the application of lime.

It is well known that certain plants will only grow on acid soils, while others will only thrive on alkaline. However, fertilizers may also change other properties of the soil, including the populations of small organisms. This is most noticeable with the application of well-rotted compost or farmyard manure, the huge addition of organic matter encouraging all forms of invertebrate life, especially earthworms. As was described in Chapter 5, such populations affect the water-holding capacity and drainage of the soil, as well as its workability. It may not be possible to make large changes of soil pH over the whole garden, but it can still be done in particular areas.

So, frosts, wind and ambient temperatures permitting, it is possible to grow a wide variety of plant species in most gardens and, as explained in Chapter 7, the plants grown can have a big effect on the animal populations. This is especially so for butterflies, moths, hover-flies, bees, wasps and a variety of beetles, most of which add interest, colour and movement, and many of which are beneficial in terms of pest control.

Uses of plant competition

As all gardeners know, plants are often very competitive – for light, nutrients or water – and will try to crowd each other out in a variety of ways. It is possible to use selected plant species to control others, and some can be deliberately used to suppress weeds.

Stinging nettles are a good example of a relatively unattractive plant species that, once established, is extremely difficult to get rid of. Their tough yellow roots will travel many metres under plastic or paper mulch, to pop up a shoot wherever a gap is found. They seem to be able to withstand repeated cutting and start growth very early in the season: indeed, new shoots can be found in midwinter. However, the lungwort (*Pulmonaria officinalis*), which has attractive foliage and flowers, can be used to suppress them. Lungworts grow vigorously and are readily transplanted, using rooted extensions of the plant that appear to grow during most of the spring, summer and autumn. I have found that clumps measuring about 15 cm (6 in) across will increase some tenfold within one season and thus occupy ground very quickly. They develop into dense patches which appear to exclude everything else, including nettles, even on ground previously full of these weeds. The plants are easily uprooted and can be dug up and planted or, as I have often done, simply dumped on the area to be covered. Unless the weather is extremely dry, they just carry on growing. All that is necessary is to cut or, better, root out the nettles before planting and then once or twice subsequently, between the clumps of lungwort. Within one season, a stage is reached where it is only necessary to pull out the occasional nettle stem.

Periwinkle (*Vinca major*), another spreading plant with attractive flowers, also has a considerable capacity to cover the ground and, with a little, but diminishing, help, will even crowd out blackberry as well. However, unlike lungwort, it is difficult to uproot and thus to eradicate if it gets out of hand. Both may try to take over the garden but lungwort is easy to control.

Of course, not all species will grow vigorously in all conditions but the range of usable competitors may be larger than we suppose and would be worth exploring. Examples of other garden plants that are suitable for ground-cover are given in Table 8.3

Table 8.3 Examples of ground-cover plants

Species	Growth form
Cotoneaster spp.	Prostrate or dwarf shrub
Euonymus 'Darts Blanket'	Prostrate shrub
Hedera helix 'Hibernica'	Woody climber or trailer
Lonicera pileata	Shrub
Rubus tricolor	Scrambler
Juniperus communis	Prostrate shrub
Alchemilla mollis	Herbaceous
Geranium macrorrhizum	Semi-evergreen herbaceous

9 Water in the Garden

To many people, an area of water adds a peaceful dimension to the garden as well as making an interesting feature. Depending on the size of the pond (or lake!), and whether it is associated with a bog garden, it allows a whole new range of plants to be grown. Running water also adds special sound effects, which most people find attractive, but this requires some fall of water, over a weir or strong shallows as a waterfall, or from a fountain. Relatively few gardens have their own stream running through them, but when they do, this allows a wide range of possibilities, for falls, deep and shallow areas, pools and boggy areas. Water always greatly increases the natural history interest of a garden as it attracts many visitors, especially the following.

Birds

Birds visit to drink and bathe, and to feed. Blackbirds seem to do the most bathing but the use birds can make of water for this purpose depends upon the provision of shallow enough areas in which they can stand (2–5 cm/³/4–2 in) – at the edges, on flat stones or bricks, on island edges, or on wooden ramps (also needed for species that need to get in and out of the water without flying).

Many bird species visit to drink, including wood-pigeons, robins, thrushes and blackbirds. Those that feed round the edges include ducks doing so from the water and wrens creeping round on even rather insecure vegetation.

Birds feeding on the contents of the pond include mallards (even on quite small ponds of only 5 x 1.5 m/16 x 5 ft) eating mainly insects, tadpoles and snails; moorhens, eating insects and duckweed; and coots, eating pond weed. If the pond is big enough these species may also nest, on the bank or on islands (mallard) or on nests anchored on tree branches trailing in the water (coots) or on clumps of vegetation, especially rushes (moorhens, which will even bend over the rushes to form a thin roof).

Birds also visit to collect mud for nesting, especially house martins and thrushes. However, the likelihood of birds visiting a garden is greatly affected by the amount of disturbance by pets as well as people.

Insects

Many of the pond inhabitants fly in and out, staying for days or weeks. These include the larger water beetles, water-boatmen and pond-skaters.

Insects that come to drink include butterflies, needing the minerals as well as the water (so enjoying even muddy pools), bees, some of which take water back to their developing grubs, and wasps, since the adults can only take liquid food (including jam and fruit juices).

Amphibians

Frogs, toads and newts visit in order to breed but the young may be resident for many months.

Reptiles

The grass snake is a common visitor and swims about with ease, looking for prey.

Both amphibians and reptiles benefit from gently sloping banks for access, especially if they lead to shallow water. Snakes can scale several centimetres of vertical wall to reach vegetation or use crevices that allow them to grip and even newts can climb some walls (if they are rough enough), but frogs and toads do need an easy way out.

Mammals

Mammals may visit to drink, including foxes, squirrels and

hedgehogs, but they are not often seen doing it. For some purposes, such as drinking, almost any patch of water will serve, providing it is accessible. There is a danger that animals, especially hedgehogs, may fall in and be unable to get out again. This can easily be overcome in ponds by providing sloping or stepped 'exits', but more ingenuity is required to solve the problem in the case of a swimming pool.

For visitors with rather more extensive purposes, however, ponds vary in their attractiveness mainly because of what is in the water – although edges are also important.

Inhabitants of the pond

Very few patches of water can support animal life if there is no plant life, although the plants may be very small and not visible to the unaided eye.

The exceptions are pools and ditches that contain decaying leaves and other plant residues. Minute animals may live on these residues and a whole food chain (or web) may be constructed on that base, with larger animals feeding on the small ones. This is even true for water-filled tree holes, quite small in volume, which may contain mosquito and midge larvae, beetles and hover-fly larvae.

In general, plants are needed to maintain an adequate oxygen content. However, not all pond animals need to absorb oxygen from the water (see Table 9.1): there are many that simply surface to breathe air.

Plants of the pond

Plants provide oxygen, mechanical support for some aquatic animals, sites for egg-laying, shade, shelter and a source of food. However, surprisingly few animals actually consume aquatic vegetation, other than algae and the microscopic plants.

The fringes of the pond, and often an associated swamp zone, contain a whole range of marsh plants (see 'A Bog Garden' in Chapter 11).

Table 9.1 Oxygen supply to pond animals

Absorption from the water	Breathing air
Fish	Water spiders
Newt larvae	Newt adults
Tadpoles	Frogs
Beetle larvae	Adult beetles
Daphnia	Drone-fly larvae
Cyclops	Backswimmers
Caddis larvae	Water-boatmen
Pond snails	
Freshwater mussel	
Dragonfly nymphs	

Table 9.2 Floating plants with roots

White water-lily	*Nymphaea alba*	Rhizomes anchored in the bottom mud
Yellow water-lily	*Nuphar lutea*	Rhizomes anchored in the bottom mud
Amphibious bistort	*Polygonum amphibium*	Has aquatic and terrestrial forms
Water-crowfoot	*Ranunculus* spp.	Snowy white flowers borne above the water
Broad-leaved pondweed	*Potamogeton natans*	Like most such plants, has both floating pondweed and submerged leaves
Common water-starwort	*Callitriche stagnalis*	Rather loose root attachment – sometimes a floating mass

Floating plants

In the water itself, there are plants with floating leaves (see Table 9.2), but often rooted in the mud; free-floating plants (see Table 9.3) which are either rootless or with roots that simply hang loosely in the water; and algae (see Box 9.1).

Box 9.1 Algae

These are the simplest forms of plant life, most common in aquatic conditions, where they occur in vast numbers. The largest are the seaweeds. In ponds they are either very small (pin-head size or less) or consist of very fine filaments. They are not usually differentiated into leaves or roots.

When the water of a pond turns green, it is usually due to millions of single-celled algae, such as *Chlamydomonas* spp., which mainly multiply by division of their motile, ovoid cells. Other species form colonies, with the cells packed tightly together. *Volvox* spp. cells form a hollow sphere, about 0.5 mm across, which have whip-like flagellae that enable them to move slowly through the water.

The least desirable species are *Spirogyra* spp., with their well-known green filaments forming soft, hair-like floating masses, commonly known as blanket weed. Each strand is made up of a single row of cylindrical cells joined end to end: under a microscope the chloroplasts can be seen as spiral bands. Although it clogs up the pond, even growing great tufts on living snail shells and forming mats round other pond weeds, it does provide food and shelter for small animals, such as baby snails and dragonfly nymphs, and newts will lay their eggs in it – if other plants are not available.

The most common of the free-floating plants is probably common duckweed (*Lemna minor*) with round or egg-shaped fronds, each with a single root hanging from the underside. The fronds are really swollen stems, rather than leaves. The greater duckweed (*Lemna polyrhiza*) has larger, circular fronds, green above and violet or reddish on the underside and with a tuft of roots. The ivy-leaved duckweed (*Lemna trisulca*) stays submerged except during flowering. The extraordinary growth potential of duckweed is described in Chapter 3 (and Box 3.9).

The dominant garden aquatic plant with floating leaves is the water-lily, of which there are several species, adapted to different depths of water. There are now many different colours of flower but the two main species are the white water-lily (*Nymphaea alba*) and the yellow water-lily or brandy-bottle (*Nuphar lutea*). The white water-lily lives in fairly deep water and has a stout rooting rhizome which anchors the plant in the mud at the bottom of the pond; the yellow water-lily tends to live in even deeper water and the rhizomes may reach 3 m (10 ft) in length.

Water-lily leaves float flat on the surface, although, when crowded, some rise up over others. They have stomata (for gaseous exchanges) on their upper surface only (see Box 3.3 for details of stomata). Sometimes the leaves are underwater, especially initially, and these contribute oxygen to the water, which the floating leaves do not.

Lily leaves provide resting places for small amphibians and emerging dragonflies as well as shelter for small animals. Very importantly, they provide excellent sites for snail eggs (see Box 4.6) on the underside, and a source of food for larvae of aquatic beetles and the brown china mark moth (*Nymphula nympheata*). The latter is a most extraordinary feature of pond life that simply passes unnoticed by most people. Once observed, however, like so much natural history, it is almost impossible to ignore.

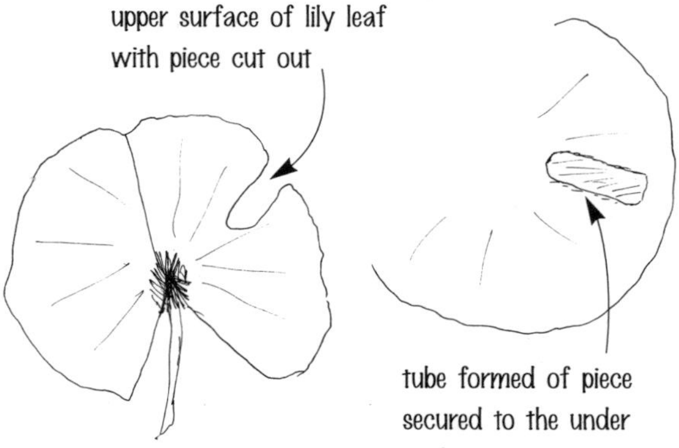

The female moth lays her eggs on the undersides of lily leaves by curling her abdomen round the edge of the leaf. Immediately after hatching the newly emerged larvae live in the water, absorbing oxygen through the skin. They are covered with unwettable hairs and grow to about 20 mm (3/4 in) in length. They make oval-shaped holes (about 25 mm/1 in long) in water-lily leaves and these are a very visible clue to their presence of the caterpillars. These oval pieces (see Figure 9.1) are fastened with

upper surface of lily leaf with piece cut out

tube formed of piece secured to the under surface

Figure 9.1 Signs of china mark moth

silk to the undersides of the leaves (but not necessarily the ones from which they were cut).

The larvae live in a trapped air space within this oval capsule and emerge at night to feed on the edges of the leaf, shown by irregular margins. Some larvae actually stick two oval pieces together and fasten this capsule to the underside of a lily leaf by one edge or end. Furthermore, the larvae can move about, towing the whole cover or capsule behind them.

It is extraordinary how such an obvious feature as the oval holes in the leaves are simply not noticed, and if they are, it is simply thought that, 'Something must be eating it.' Yet turning over a few leaves will easily reveal the capsules. Even so, few people would expect the cause to be a moth and it raises interesting questions as to how the moth finally emerges from the pupa to fly away.

Figure 9.2 Water-starwort

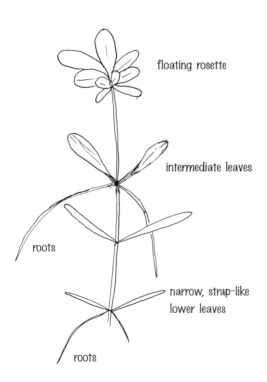

floating rosette

intermediate leaves

roots

narrow, strap-like lower leaves

roots

Submerged pond plants

Submerged plants tend to have weak stems and numerous small, translucent leaves. Some of them, however, project their flowers above the surface. Two of the most common and, from a natural history point of view, most interesting, are the common water-starwort (*Callitriche stagnalis*) and the Canadian waterweed (*Elodea canadensis*).

The common water-starwort is loosely rooted to the mud at the bottom of the pond and, in the winter, sinks to the bottom and remains there until the spring. It then produces a long, pale, thin stem with narrow, strap-like leaves. Nearer to the surface, these become spoon-shaped and then, at the surface, the leaves form floating green rosettes (see Figure 9.2).

Many small animals (for example the freshwater shrimp, *Gammarus pulex*) live among the starwort clumps, which can be quite dense, but the most impressive feature is the use of starwort leaves by the smooth newt, as a repository for its eggs (see Box 9.2).

Box 9.2 Newt egg deposition

Figure 9.2 shows normally growing leaves of the common water-starwort and it is the intermediate (spoon-shaped) leaves that are often used by female smooth newts to lay their eggs on. The newt grasps a leaf with her hind legs, folds it and lays an egg in the fold, as shown (right).

The egg is embedded in a sticky jelly which glues the folded leaf down. This is not normally visible from above the surface, but what can easily be seen is the visible changed leaf outline. This is so marked that it is quite possible to visit a pond in the spring and spot the leaves with newt eggs. The appearance from above is shown (right).

If the folded leaf is removed and kept in water, the egg will hatch but before that occurs, since the egg is transparent, the developing larva can be seen. Just before hatching, its gills can be seen and it wriggles about (below).

If such leaves are not available, eggs may be laid in, for example, blanket weed.

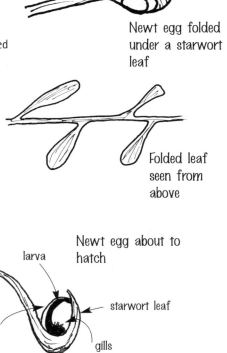

Newt egg folded under a starwort leaf

Folded leaf seen from above

Newt egg about to hatch

larva

egg

starwort leaf

gills

Canadian pondweed is a common weed of stagnant or slow-running water and is also commonly used in aquaria. It is one of the most effective oxygenators and, in sunny conditions, bubbles of oxygen can be seen rising in streams from the ovate, stalkless, green leaves (see Figure 9.3). Although able to produce flowers and seeds, reproduction is usually by fragmentation. The plant produces long roots from any part of the stem and these grow in the bottom mud, but any piece of the rather brittle, translucent stems will generate a whole new plant.

Figure 9.3 Canadian pondweed

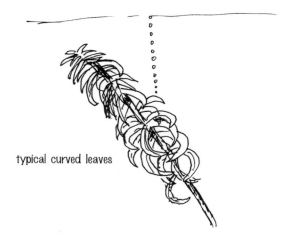

leaf emitting a thin stream of bubbles of oxygen in sunlight

typical curved leaves

Plants of the pond edge

There are, of course, many other species of plant in and around ponds but one other category is important, because of its significance to those animals (mainly insects) which spend their larval lives under water but their adult lives in a non-aquatic phase. These are the edge plants, which are mainly vertical. The significance to the insects is that the leaves and stems are used by the larvae during their emergence, the most spectacular being the dragonflies (see Box 9.3).

A great variety of plants will serve this purpose and, if no vertical plants are available, dragonfly nymphs will also climb up on to lily

Box 9.3 Emergence of dragonflies

There are roughly 43 species of dragonflies and damselflies in the British Isles (see table for examples). They vary in size and colour but most are spectacular, in bright, often metallic colours.

Sub-order	Family	Species	Common name	Colour	Size (mm)*
Anisoptera	*Aeshnidae*	*Aeshna cyanea*	Southern aeshna (a hawker dragonfly)	Initially yellow and black, later green and blue	71–76
Anisoptera	*Libellulidae*	*Libellula depressa*	Broad-bodied libellula (a darter dragonfly)	Blue with yellow spots (males)	44–50
Zygoptera	*Lestidae*	*Lestes sponsa*	Green lestes (a damselfly)	Emerald	33–40

* 25 mm = 1 inch

The adults can fly forwards, sideways and even backwards, catching their prey on the wing. They are capable of speeds of 40–48 km/h (25–30 mph). They also mate (mainly) on the wing and lay their eggs in or on the water. These hatch to produce larvae (called nymphs in the case of dragonflies), which are ferocious predators on other aquatic creatures. Examples are shown below.

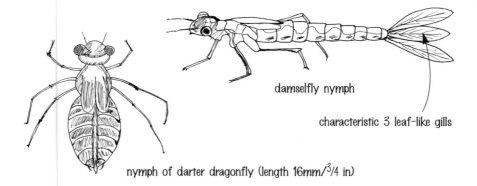

damselfly nymph

characteristic 3 leaf-like gills

nymph of darter dragonfly (length 16mm/³/4 in)

These nymphs spend up to three years in the water, absorbing oxygen from it, and show no trace of the gaudy colours that they will display as adults. When the time comes to emerge, they climb out of the water and up a stem or leaf. This may happen fairly early on a summer's morning or, in some species, at night, and they need a fine, dry period (how do these nymphs know when to emerge?).

The crumpled adult emerges through a hole in the upper part of the thorax, leaving behind the complete larval skin, legs, eyes and all. The emerged adult may climb up further, or rest on the discarded skin, while it swells to its full size, pumps fluid into its wings to expand them before they harden, and dries out, the whole process taking about $1^1/2$ hours.

All this is easily observed, as this is a time when the insects are immobile. One astonishing feature is that the adult may be more than twice as big as the nymph from which it emerged. For example, I have measured a libellula adult at 40 mm ($1^1/2$ in) in length (wing span 60 mm/$2^1/2$ in) immediately after emerging from a nymphal case of 24 mm (1 in), and a 32 mm ($1^1/4$ in) damselfly adult emerging from a 12 mm ($^1/2$ in) case. It is, of course, very vulnerable at this time and, indeed, during its first fluttering flight: many are picked off by birds at this stage.

The contrast between adult and nymph is considerable, yet the one actually emerges from the other. Caterpillars of butterflies and moths are also quite unlike the adults but they go through a total bodily reorganization within the pupa. The main function of the adults is to mate and reproduce and their lives are comparatively short (a few weeks or months).

As with so many insects, it raises an interesting question as to which phase really constitutes the individual: a question even more sharply focused in the case of mayflies, where the adult has no mouthparts for feeding and only lives for a few hours.

---

leaves or up the walls of the pond. However, the ideal plants are bulrush (*Typha latifolia*), yellow flag or yellow iris (*Iris pseudacorus*) and the rushes (*Juncus* spp.). Other common edge plants are listed in Table 9.4.

Many of them grow at tremendous rates, mainly because water and nutrients are not normally limiting; as a result, they may even take over the whole pond – if it is shallow enough. Mostly such plants spread in all directions into the water, often by means of very thick, tough rhizomes (yellow flag, bulrush, bog arum and bur-reed). Others, such as the rushes, form large tussocks, which are used by moorhens as nesting sites. The nest may be quite substantial and the

Table 9.4 Plants of the pond edge

Reed sweet-grass	*Glyceria maxima*	Up to 2 m (6^1/$_2$ ft) tall, yellowish-green. Leaves (with cutting edges)
Common reed	*Phragmites australis*	1–4 m (3^1/$_4$–13 ft) high – a true grass, plume-like flowers
Great pond sedge	*Carex riparia*	1–1.6 m (3^1/$_4$–5^1/$_4$ ft) tall, like all sedges has flower stems that are triangular in cross-section
Bulrush	*Typha latifolia*	Up to 2 m (6^1/$_2$ ft) tall, flowers in spikes – pale, male flowers above, dark brown female flowers beneath
Bog arum	*Calla palustris*	Leathery, heart-shaped leaves on long stalks
Rushes	*Juncus* spp.	Smooth, hairless leaves and stalks, round in cross-section, filled with pith, pointed
Water mint	*Mentha aquatica*	Leaves strongly smelling of mint, especially when crushed, stems four-sided, globular lilac-coloured flower heads
Common persicaria (redshank)	*Polygonum persicaria*	Purplish-red stems swollen at nodes, with spear-shaped leaves, flowers pink
Marsh horsetail	*Equisetum palustre*	60 cm (24 in) tall, grooved stems with encircling leaves at nodes
Kingcup (marsh marigold)	*Caltha palustris*	Large, buttercup-like flowers, long stalked leaves carried above the water
Yellow flag (iris)	*Iris pseudacorus*	Sword-shaped leaves, 50–100 cm (1^3/$_4$–3^1/$_4$ ft) tall, typical (yellow) iris flower

roof that is often made by the bird bending some of the rush stems over helps to conceal the eggs viewed from above. The underwater parts of these plants afford protection for small creatures and provide surfaces for the growth of algae on which snails and other species feed.

Animals of the pond

The animals that live in the pond, as opposed to visitors, may nevertheless not spend their whole lives there. Table 9.5 illustrates the main (common) species that use the pond only for reproduction, where this phase is a relatively small part of their lives. However, it could also be argued that a whole range of, chiefly, insects, such as the mayfly, also use the pond only for reproduction – but it is the adult (non-aquatic) phase that lasts only a small proportion of their lives. Table 9.6 lists examples of these animals, the larval stages of which are major and characteristic inhabitants of ponds.

Table 9.5 Animals that use water only for reproduction

		Lifespan* Tadpole	Adult
Frogs	*Rana temporaria* (common frog)	70+ days	up to 12 yrs
Toads	*Bufo bufo*	60–100 days (common toad)	up to 40 yrs
	Bufo calamita (natterjack)	42–60 days	up to 15 yrs
Newts	*Triturus vulgaris* (smooth newt)	$3^{1}/2$–4 months	up to 6 yrs
	Triturus cristatus (great crested newt)	5–6 months	up to 10 yrs

* The life-span for adults is for known individual cases: the average will be much less, even for survivors from predators and diseases.

Discovering the pond inhabitants

Lists of animals and plants are useful indicators of what species are likely to be present, but they tell you little about how to discover

Table 9.6 Animals with long larval stages in the water

Insects	Life–span Larvae	Adult
Dragonflies	2–3 yrs	2–3 months
Mayflies	1 yr	c. 1 day
Caddis flies	c. 1 yr	hours or days
Phantom midge	1 yr	hours or days
China mark moth	c. 1 yr	3–4 months

them and convey nothing of the excitement of finding them.

To some extent, the animals in a pond depend upon the age of the pond and the time of year when it was established. In the spring and summer, mosquito larvae may appear within days but newts and frogs may take one or more years. For most of the plants, and certainly the larger ones, their presence or absence is easily perceived, but this may not be true of the smaller ones and not all are present at all times of the year.

Most of the edge plants grow much like other garden plants. Some of the prettiest are not confined to pond edges, including the spring blooms of the primrose, cowslip and fritillary, and many of the ferns, for example hart's tongue (*Phyllitis scolopendrium*) and the royal fern (*Osmunda regalis*), look well by water but grow just as well elsewhere.

The aquatic species mostly die down during the winter and appear again the following spring. This is very noticeable, for example, with the pale green water-starwort (*Callitriche stagnalis*), which, however prominent during the summer, seems to have totally disappeared in the winter. Similarly with the duckweeds; the entire pond surface may be covered by a thick mat of duckweed during the summer but only small frond remnants (full of starch) may survive at the bottom of the pond during winter. In the spring, the starch is used up and they rise to the surface, where they produce small green fronds and hanging roots. At first sight, the mat of duckweed looks rather uninteresting but it probably consists of several species of duckweed (see Table 9.3), each with a characteristic number of roots and with fronds busy dividing up to produce new plants (see Box 3.9). Furthermore, on separation, some of these species look totally different, such as the ivy-leaved duckweed (*Lemna trisulca*), which cannot really be seen clearly when mixed in with other species (see Figure 9.4).

Figure 9.4 Ivy-leaved duckweed

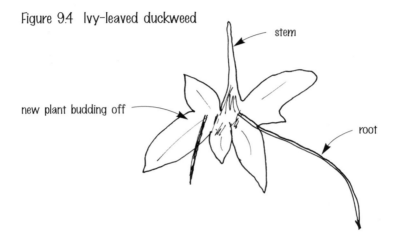

stem

new plant budding off

root

Among this mass of tiny plants there are often little animals, some microscopic (for example *Hydra* spp.), some young stages (for example frogs and pond snails), some adults just coming up for air (for example beetles, water boatmen), but also some case-building larvae. The most common of these are caddis-fly larvae (see Box 9.4) and the larvae of the small china mark moth (*Cataclysta lemnata*), which constructs a rather loose case from duckweed fronds.

If the surface of the water is clear, or nearly so, the most obvious insects will probably be easily seen. Pond-skaters (*Gerris* spp.) and whirligig beetles (*Gyrinus* spp.) both live on material on the surface, and pond-skaters will rush towards any insect that falls into the water and becomes trapped by the surface tension. (One of the consequences of very small size is that the surface tension of water may be too powerful to break free from.)

Pond-skaters appear to skate on the surface, 'rowing' along on feet with unwettable hairs, whereas whirligig beetles gyrate very rapidly, without visible leg action. Both breed in the water but can easily fly

Box 9.4 Caddis-fly larvae

Caddis flies (*Trichoptera*) are closely related to butterflies and moths but the
wings are hairy – not covered with scales. There are about 185 species in the UK
and all have aquatic larvae. These are notable because they live inside tubular
cases, constructed from a wide variety of materials (for example sand, weed, dead
leaves, small sticks, pieces of vegetation) that tend to be characteristic of the
species (see below). *Limnophilus flavicornis*, for example, builds its case out of
small, flat, empty snail shells. The larvae are secured at the rear with a pair of
hooks and the tough brown head end protrudes at the front for feeding and
towing the case along.

Caddis larval cases

snail shells   pieces of leaf   thin blades of   dead leaves
                 and bark   water weed

The larval stage lasts a year and the larvae and their cases are up to 2 cm ($3/4$ in)
long, so they are quite easy to see, especially if they use sizable dead leaves – but
only when they move. Otherwise they are well camouflaged. The adults live for
only about a month.

---

away to another pond. They may therefore appear and disappear
quite suddenly, but this also means that they can arrive at a new
pond within weeks of its establishment, partly because their source of
food falls into water at a rate that has little to do with how long the
water has been there.

However unappealing the life-style of the surface feeders strikes you, it is a form of recycling of dead bodies and there is no doubt that dead and dying creatures on or in the water (earthworms and slugs, as well as moths, flies and grasshoppers) detract markedly from its attractiveness to us. Thus, these tidiers-up of the environment serve a useful purpose – just like those that scavenge on the roads or bury carcasses on land.

Snails are not really surface-dwellers but will often travel upside down in the water but at the surface, harvesting material from the surface film – but from underneath!

In addition to those that live on the surface, there are a number of creatures that come up periodically for air, sometimes to gulp a fresh supply (for example newts) and sometimes to trap air under their wing cases (for example water beetles) or amongst stiff hairs on the body or legs (for example water-boatmen). Simply watching the surface for a time will therefore reveal (eventually!) all those who live below the surface or in the mud but who need to breathe air.

This also applies to the larvae of mosquitoes (see Box 9.5), some of the first inhabitants to arrive in a new source of water (including a water butt or even a pool in the angle between branches of a tree). They are very noticeable because of their vigorous wriggling, but the eggs are generally ignored. Not only that, but who ever asks what makes the eggs unwettable – and therefore unsinkable? And would you not think that that might even be useful information?

Box 9.5 Mosquito larvae

There are some 36 species of mosquito in the UK and only some of them pester humans; others suck blood from other mammals, birds, reptiles or even frogs. Only the females suck blood; the males feed on nectar.

The eggs are laid on the water and, in the case of one our commonest mosquitoes, *Culex pipiens*, produce spectacular unsinkable rafts of up to 300 conical eggs (see Box 4.6). Each larva hatches through a trap door at the bottom of the egg and drops straight down into the water. The larvae wriggle up to the surface to collect air, and then down again when disturbed, feeding on minute particles of suspended matter.

After a few days, the larval skin splits and a pupal stage emerges: this has a large head and thorax, containing an air space for buoyancy. Eventually, the pupal skin splits at the surface and a new adult emerges and, when the wings have hardened, flies off.

Not all species can transmit malaria: *Culex* species cannot, but some *Anopheles* species can. Both are found in the UK. They can be distinguished very easily, both in the larval and adult phase. *Culex* species adults rest with the body parallel to the surface, whereas *Anopheles* species rest with the head down and the abdomen inclined upwards (see below). *Culex* eggs form a raft and the larvae hang upside down almost vertically from the surface. *Anopheles* lays single eggs and the larvae rest parallel to the water surface.

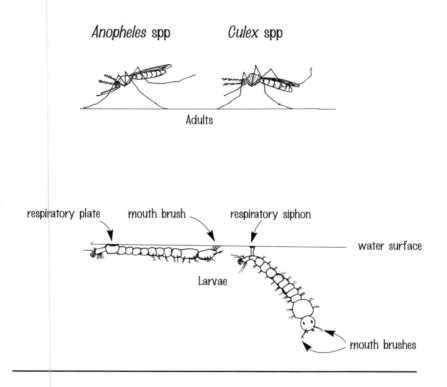

Anopheles spp   *Culex* spp

Adults

respiratory plate   mouth brush   respiratory siphon

water surface

Larvae

mouth brushes

A whole range of beetles live in the water (see Table 9.7) and come to the surface for air, and they include two species that are among our largest insects. Other aquatic insects include the larvae of true flies (*Diptera*) and a number of bugs (*Hemiptera*). Although many insects and other small invertebrates are commonly referred to as 'bugs', entomologically speaking the term is only used for this family of insects, such as greenfly, characterized by their possession of piercing and sucking mouthparts. They include the pond-skaters and the more sedate water measurers (*Hydrometridae*), the water scorpions – only alarming to other pond creatures – and the water-boatmen.

Table 9.7 Aquatic beetles

Common name	Latin name	Length (mm)*	Food	Larvae
Whirligig beetles	*Gyrinidae*	4–20 mm (varying with species)	*Chironomus* spp. (midge larvae)	15 mm 8 segments with gills
Great silver water beetle	*Hydrophilus piceus*	50 mm	plants (algae)	Carnivorous (on snails)
Furrowed acilius	*Acilius sulcatus*	16 mm	small insects and crustaceans	Very long first segment, so the head looks as if it is on a long neck
The great diving beetle	*Dytiscus marginalis*	35 mm	insects, tadpoles, small fish	Voracious predator, active summer, feeds on small animals, 50 mm

* 25 mm = 1 in

There are two kinds of the latter, the so-called backswimmers (*Notonectidae*) that swim upside down and feed mainly on insects falling into the water, and the *Corixidae*, which swim the right way up and feed on plants. The backswimmers are larger (15 mm/½ in) than the others and naturally float, whereas the others sink when they stop 'rowing' with their powerful legs.

One of the fascinating and surprising features of the backswimmers is their coloration. Most animals tend to be darker above than below, which is better for camouflage, but, in the backswimmers, this is reversed. Thus the underside, which is what you see, is dark grey and it hardly occurs to you that it is not the same underneath (that is, on its upper surface). However, if you turn it over (so that it is the right way up!), you will find that its upper side is a light greenish colour, which would stand out markedly if it swam the right way up. Note that this has to be done with some care as it can give you a painful stab with its pointed mouthparts.

Many of the pond inhabitants feed on small crustaceans, such as *Daphnia* and *Cyclops* (see Figure 9.5), and others forage in the mud for freshwater shrimps, bloodworms (see Box 9.6) and other small creatures, some of which make tubes of mud particles or of duckweed fronds.

Figure 9.3

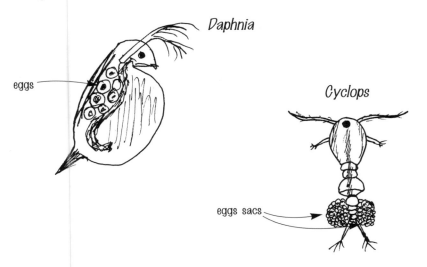

Gazing into the water and focusing at different levels soon reveals an astonishing range of life forms, but they do vary quite rapidly, some species showing high population density at one time and others at other times – not just at different seasons but changing over a matter of weeks, almost disappearing and then coming back again.

This applies to crustaceans (*Cyclops* and *Daphnia*), which are more readily seen if a white tray or dish is placed horizontally below the surface. This will often reveal a whole world of life that otherwise we

---

Box 9.6 Bloodworms

In the muddy deposits at the bottom of sluggish streams, water-butts or stagnant pools are found blood-red worm-like creatures (known as 'bloodworms') that are actually the larvae of midges (*Chironomus* spp.). When fully grown they are up to 2.5 cm (1 in) in length and they live in (usually) vertical tubes made of debris held together by their saliva.

The red colour is actually due to haemoglobin (as in our own blood), which acts as an oxygen carrier. This is a relatively rare occurrence, found in creatures living in water with a low oxygen content. It also occurs in *Daphnia*, the worm *Tubifex* and *Planorbis* snails, under these conditions.

The midge lays her eggs in masses of gelatinous micro-algae on the water surface, but they are transparent and very hard to see.

'see through'. Not only can many more *Daphnia* be seen, including young ones, but the egg sacs carried by the female *Cyclops* are also clearly visible (see Figure 9.5).

In addition, the transparent, horizontal larvae of the well-named phantom midge (*Chaoborus crystallinas*) may suddenly come into view. Although 13-15 mm (½ in) in length, they are very easily overlooked. Against a dark background, they can best be seen by shining a torch at an angle. These phantom midge larvae are quite unlike any others (see Figure 9.6). There is a hydrostatic (buoyancy) organ at each end and two black eyes can be clearly seen. They appear to lie still in the water and then, suddenly, they give a flick and reappear, motionless again, a short distance away. They are 'active' even at very low temperatures and feed on small insects and crustaceans. A number of other water creatures may be observed at night, partly because they are more active and partly because torchlight does not seem to disturb them (and reflection off the surface is not a problem).

Daphnia and *Cyclops* feed on very small organisms, including single-celled algae. Among these are the flagellates, so-called because they propel themselves along using a whip-like tail. It has recently been found that these microscopic creatures can sense the presence of water fleas and react by burying themselves in the sediment at the bottom of the water.

Figure 9.6   Phantom midge larva (1 cm/1 1/2 in)

side view

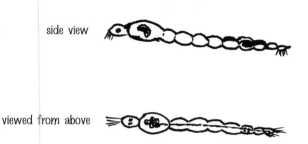

viewed from above

   This illustrates how easy it is to underestimate the awareness of even lowly organisms to their environment. They can do things that we cannot: it adds to the wonder inherent in natural history and reinforces the thought that we should continually ask (in some awe): 'How do they do that?'

10 Visitors

One of the pleasures of a gardener is to show visitors around and this illustrates very well the argument, put forward in Chapter 1, that most garden tours consist of visiting what is known to be there. Most of it is deliberately put there, planted or placed, and many gardeners love re-creating parts of the garden, moving plants and introducing new ones. In the eyes of the gardener, this is what most gardens are for. So visitors are shown all these features, which to them may offer the delight of discovery.

Of course, gardens change daily and seasonally, so they do not become boring to the gardener who sees them every day. There is also a pleasure in anticipation – of seedlings emerging, flowers blooming, changes in leaf colour and, in some cases, seed formation. But there are also natural visitors not always expected, not always welcome and, mostly, simply not known about. Such visitors are almost entirely animals, since plants do not move about and the parts that do, such as seeds and spores, can hardly be said to visit: they merely arrive and are mostly unwelcome.

Walled gardens may keep out most of the non-flying animals but fences usually make little difference unless they allow no access points at all. Let us consider the main visitors and why they come, under the headings of the main animal groups.

Mammals

The largest wild mammalian visitors to gardens are deer: in the UK these are mostly the small muntjak in urban areas, but roe and fallow deer may visit in rural districts. They are all easily recognized, though only occasionally seen, and sometimes do considerable damage.

Badgers and foxes are frequent nocturnal visitors to some gardens, foxes being now very common in urban areas, attracted by food wastes and sometimes actually living under a building unbeknownst to the occupier. Both are animals that may range quite widely and both eat earthworms in considerable numbers. In general, they do no harm, although badgers may create gaps in fences to provide regular access and foxes may cause havoc in hen-houses, if they can get into them. Both tend to follow well-worn tracks and these may be the only signs you ever see of their presence.

A visitor commonly regarded as a pest is the grey squirrel, but this is mainly due to its habit of stripping bark off young trees and its impact on most garden vegetation is slight. However, there is a common antipathy to creatures with a reputation for stealing eggs or nestlings (see Box 10.1).

Hedgehogs may be visitors (with a range of 0.5–10 ha/1¼–25 acres or more) but may also be residents, feeding mainly on pests (see Box 10.2). Below hedgehog size (for example mice and voles), mammals tend to be residents, unless the garden is very small, except for bats

---

Box 10.1 Destroyers of young

Because of our protective instincts with regard to the young – though we do not extend this to blowfly maggots, for example – we react unfavourably to the whole idea of stealing of eggs or the destruction of the young: indeed, we do not really approve of one bird stealing material from another's nest – although this often happens. This is quite illogical, of course, since most animals reproduce at rates that would swamp the world if all the young survived (see Chapters 4 and 7). It is also based on a romantic rather than a realistic view of nature, because, in fact, the survival of all carnivorous animals depends upon them eating others.

The main stealers of birds' eggs are grey squirrels, magpies, crows, jays and hedgehogs. Magpies and jays often concentrate on the eggs of wood-pigeons – frequently considered to be a pest. Cuckoos also destroy the eggs and young of the species they exploit, but this is done by the developing young cuckoos, which even have a structural adaptation (a hollow at the back of the neck/shoulder region) that allows them to eject rival eggs.

The young of mammals (for example rabbits, mice, voles) are eaten by stoats, weasels and snakes, and the young of insects (for example caterpillars) are eaten by insectivorous birds, quite apart from the depredations of parasites.

(see Boxes 10.3 and 10.4). Moles, however, may also be visitors, since their underground tunnels do not recognize boundaries (see Chapter 5).

Box 10.2 Hedgehogs

The hedgehog (*Erinaceus europaeus*), sometimes called the urchin or hedgepig, is familiar to everyone. Unfortunately, its instinctive defensive reaction, to roll itself into a ball, is inappropriate for traffic hazards and most hedgehogs are seen as sad victims of road accidents.

They are nocturnal and rest during the day under dead leaves or in hedgerows, where it is said that they can sometimes be heard snoring. Indeed, they are more often heard, snuffling about in the night, than seen. They live on snails, slugs, worms, insects and even mice, rats and frogs, and adults are really quite big (for example >25 cm/10 in) and weigh about 600 g ($1^{1}/4$ lb) or more.

The hedgehog is one of the true hibernators, living off its stored fat, and thus stores no food, as do the intermittent hibernators, such as dormice. It has poor eyesight but an acute sense of smell, and can climb well, its spines (of which it has about 6000) cushioning it if it falls.

Hedgehogs produce four to six young, which have pale, soft spines, mainly in early summer.

Box 10.3 Bats

Bats belong to the Order *Chiroptera*, of which there are 32 European species, and are all mammals – the only flying mammals in the UK. The leathery wings or flight membranes are supported by extensions of the finger bones and backward-bending knees. They live in colonies, hanging upside-down from rafters in roof-spaces and similar habitats, and communicate by high-pitched squeaks and clicks, mostly inaudible to people (especially older people) and different from their echolocation calls. The frequency and other characteristics of their sounds can be picked up by a 'bat detector' and used to identify bats, at least into groups. Some moths can detect bat noise and remain still to avoid capture.

The commonest, and smallest, bat in the UK is the common pipestrelle (*Pipistrellus pipistrellus*), which can be observed on warm evenings, leaving the roost about 20 minutes after sunset, and hunting for flying insects, using echolocation to find them. A bat may take as many as 3000 midges in one night.

The pipistrelle mostly roosts in houses, often in sizable colonies of about 80: it weighs about 5 g and produces tiny young, weighing not much more than 1–2 g.

Since bats are so small and can only feed when the temperature is high enough, they survive by hibernation in winter and daily torpor, when the body temperature drops to ambient (thus saving energy).

All bat species are legally protected in all EU countries (see Box 10.4). Apart from the pipistrelle, those most commonly seen tend to be the horseshoe bat (another small one – 5 g), the greater horseshoe (25 g and can live up to 30 years), the long-eared noctules which operate down to 0°C (32°F) and nest in old woodpecker holes or hollow trees, and Daubenton's bat, which always lives near water (and is a strong swimmer!) and is often seen swooping under bridges.

Box 10.4 Protected species

The following animals are protected by law in the UK at all stages of their lives. It is not permitted to catch them or interfere with them in any way.

Animal species	Comment
Stag beetle (*Lucanus cervus*)	Remember that the larvae remain unseen in rotten logs for up to 3 years
All bat species	Protection applies in all European countries
Badgers	Said to be the most protected land mammal in Europe
Red squirrels	Fully protected

Plant species

There are at least 62 fully protected species in the UK. These may not be picked, uprooted or destroyed, traded (or advertised for trade) – not even parts or derivatives. Examples are:

Some orchids

Greater yellow-rattle (*Rhinanthus serotinus*)

Lady's slipper (*Cypripedium calceolus*)

Purple spurge (*Euphorbia peplis*)

Rough marsh-mallow (*Althea hirsuta*)

Spiked speedwell (*Veronica spicata*)

Wild cotoneaster (*Cotoneaster integerrimus*)

Reptiles and amphibians

Snakes are visitors, especially grass snakes (see Box 10.5), although they are not often seen. Frogs, toads and newts may travel considerable distances to reach their favoured ponds in early spring.

Box 10.5 Snakes

There are only three species in the UK, none of which occur in Northern Ireland (nor Eire). One of them, the smooth snake (*Coronella austriaca austriaca*) does actually feel smooth, rarely exceeds 45 cm (18 in) in length, has a grey/brown background colour with dark spots, usually in pairs, and is found mainly in the New Forest and other parts of Hampshire, Dorset, Surrey and Berkshire. It is not to be confused with the similarly sized legless lizard the slow-worm (*Anguis fragilis*), which is also smooth-skinned. However, it has eyelids, which snakes do not have, and a notched rather than a forked tongue. It is especially fond of the small, greyish-white slug (*Limax agrestis*) so it ought to be one of the gardener's best friends.

Probably the most common snake in our gardens is the grass snake (*Natrix natrix helvetica*), which can grow up to 1.2 m (4 ft) in length. Characteristically, it has two patches of yellow just behind the head, giving rise to another of its names, the ringed snake, and patches of black behind those. The general colour is grey/olive-brown with black markings – dots on the back and vertical bars along the side. Food varies with size, but frogs, toads and newts are staples of the larger ones; young ones eat worms, slugs and tadpoles. It hisses but, like the smooth snake (and the slow-worm), is completely harmless. The female lays her eggs in late summer in rotting vegetation or stable manure, the heat generated assisting incubation.

The only poisonous snake is the adder (*Vipera berus berus*) or viper, which is usually about 60 cm (2 ft) long and rather thin in the body, with a short tail. The pupil of the eye is vertical, whereas in the grass snake and the slow-worm it is round. Generally brown, it usually has a dark zig-zag line down the back. It is very widespread and said to be the only British snake to be found in Scotland.

The adder mainly frequents dry areas and the eggs contain fully developed young when laid. It is not really aggressive but will bite if caught or trodden on and the venom is sufficiently serious to justify treatment (bleeding, sucking or anti-venom serum).

Birds

Unless the garden is very large, most of the birds seen are visitors and it is hard to say what a 'resident' bird is. Even the birds that nest in a garden normally collect their food over a much larger area. Some bird species are only winter visitors to the UK and some come only in the summer (see Table 10.1). The summer ones may nest and spend most of their time within a garden, for example the spotted flycatcher, which may regularly return to more or less the same nesting site each year and establish favourite perches from which to make its characteristic fly-catching forays.

Table 10.1 Seasonal bird visitors to the garden

Winter visitors	Summer visitors
Fieldfare	Swallow
Redwing	House martin
	Cuckoo
	Spotted flycatcher
	Redstart

Martins and swallows also return to the same nest-sites but they spend little time in the garden, unless it includes large stretches of water, over which they swoop to catch their prey and, in the case of house martins, collect mud for nest building. Martins are well-known for their close association with human dwellings and do not seem to be greatly troubled by human presence. Young ones can often be seen peeping out of their mud homes, so they are watching us from a very early age. Swallows build their nests, using some mud but much other material, on beams or shelf-like locations in barns and garages, provided they can have constant access.

Swallows live on flying insects and these are largely absent during the winter: this is the main reason why they migrate to warmer climes for the season. The good part of this feeding habit is that they can refuel while they fly to South Africa during the day and rest at night. These enormous distances are astonishing for such a slight bird. Swallows may live for 15 years (although only about one in five successfully complete their first migration) and during this time it has been calculated that they fly the equivalent of 100 times round the earth. Insect consumption is also impressive and our long summer days allow 2–3 broods to be produced each year, each brood consuming up to 6000 flies per day!

Winter visitors do not nest in the UK and often flock together in fields. Fieldfares and redwings do this but they may also be found (especially the latter) foraging about in gardens, like small flocks of thrushes.

Birds that are with us all the year round may nest in gardens in nest boxes (especially the tits), in odd corners (including old kettles and so on, a favourite of robins), in holes or spaces between wooden structures (for example wrens), in trees (mistle thrushes, crows, rooks, magpies) or in hedges (for example robins, hedge-sparrows, blackbirds and thrushes). Ground-nesting birds find few opportunities to nest in gardens, although mallard and pheasant may do so in large gardens without dogs or cats.

Since birds visit mainly in search of food, they can be attracted by the provision of scraps, fat, nuts and water in the winter when natural food supplies are scarce and ponds and puddles may be iced over. The plants available, especially in seed, have a considerable effect, as illustrated in Chapter 4.

Many of the common birds feed mainly on insects or other small invertebrates and are thus more attracted to gardens with high populations of these little creatures. Lawns are especially attractive to green woodpeckers (looking for ants), mistle and song thrushes and blackbirds. In search of worms, these latter species cock their heads on one side, appearing to be listening, and blackbirds may be seen stamping their feet. This is also done by gulls, to stimulate worms to rise to the surface. It resembles the old practice of 'fiddling' for worms (vibrating a stick driven into the ground) and is thought to fool the worms into thinking that it is raining.

Invertebrates

Non-flying invertebrates, such as young spiders trailing a silken thread, can be carried by the wind and very small organisms are carried on the feet of birds, but the most noticeable visiting invertebrates are the flying insects. There are huge numbers of these, of enormous variety, visiting to find a mate, to lay eggs on a suitable source of food for the larvae, to feed themselves (and, of course, to die, though that hardly constitutes the purpose of their visit!). Those that are attracted by water are dealt with in Chapter 9 and flying visitors to banks of flowers are described in Chapter 2.

The insects that come to lay their eggs are only visitors as adults and the rest of the life-cycle is 'residential', but many of the butterflies and moths may visit just to feed on nectar or find a mate. Nectar feeding is described for butterflies and moths in Box 2.5 and for bumble-bees in Box 7.1.

For moths, finding a mate is often accomplished by the secretion of pheromones (see Box 4.1) but for butterflies there is much more dependence on visual attraction and territorial behaviour. Butterflies do use scent, and this may involve both sexes, from the female to attract the male and from the male to stimulate the female. Territorial behaviour occurs in some species, with males defending a territory and chasing off other males. Some species that visit gardens may actually be visiting the country – as migrants (see Table 10.2).

Many flying insect visitors do not have a purpose for visiting a particular garden, however, and may simply be passing by. A few make their presence felt by blundering into people, windows or rooms if the window is open. These are fairly easily identified, partly by their size but also by their appearance. There are five main big ones – all beetles. The dung-beetle (*Geotrupes stercorarius*) is heavy, 2 cm (3/4 in) long and blue-black (see Table 4.1 and Box 5.2). There are two large water-beetles (see Chapter 9) that fly from one pond or lake to another, mainly at night, and may mistake the reflection from glass for a water surface.

Then, and most commonly experienced, there are the two chafers, the large cockchafer (*Melolantha melolantha*) or May-bug and the much smaller garden chafer (*Phyllopertha horticola*) or June-bug. They mostly feed on the leaves of trees and are quite harmless, but often swarm around treetops at dusk with a loud humming sound and cause alarm by bumping into people or the windows of the house.

Table 10.2 Butterfly visitors

Migrants

Migrants do not overwinter in this country and may have flown hundreds of miles to get here. Common examples are the red admiral (*Vanessa atalanta*) and the painted lady (*Vanessa cardui*). Both occasionally hibernate but rarely survive to breed. The British population thus depends on migration, largely from France and Belgium. The Camberwell beauty (*Nymphalis antiopa*) is a rare migrant, from Scandinavia.

Hibernators

Hibernators tend to appear earlier in the year. They include the peacock (*Inachis io*); the small tortoiseshell (*Aglais urticae*); the brimstone (*Gonepteryx rhamni*); and the comma (*Polygonia c-album*)

In addition to the above, which hibernate as adults, some 35 species hibernate as larvae (for example the large copper, *Lycaena dispar*), others as pupae (11) and some as eggs (9).

The monarch butterfly (*Danaus plexippus*), one of the most spectacular migratory species, is a visitor to gardens in North America.

Attracting visitors

For wildlife, there are four main attractants in a garden: food, mates, homes and shelter.

Food

Foxes, hedgehogs and some birds are examples of animals that will come for food deliberately provided and will become, if not tame, at least unafraid. They will visit regularly, often keeping to the same time. Other birds will come for food that is part of the garden (for example insects) or left untidied for them, such as seed-eating birds on seed heads and voles and mice attracted by rose hips.

Many invertebrates visit to find a food plant for their young: the stinging nettle is one such plant (see Box 10.6). Others come to feed on those that feed on the plant: for example, ladybirds and hover-fly larvae on plants with aphids. Butterflies seeking nectar are particularly attracted by plants such as buddleia, corncockle, larkspur and anchusa.

Box 10.6 Nettles and their fauna

It is well known that certain butterflies lay their eggs on the leaves of stinging nettles but there are also other insects that do this, such as aphids and the nettle weevil (*Phyllobius pomaceus*).

The red admiral is probably the best known of the butterflies but its hairy larvae, with their yellow-flashed sides, may not be very visible because they are enveloped in rolled-up leaves. The peacock is a butterfly that lays its eggs only on nettles (which it can smell with its front legs!): it lays 50–60 eggs per leaf – a total of some 500. Brachonid flies may be found on the blackish cocoons. However, the pupae of butterflies are usually found elsewhere than on the food plant if this dies down in the winter. The gold-spotted pupae of the red admiral may be found under the eaves of garden sheds and other such sheltered spots.

In total, some 107 species of insect are associated with nettles, of which 31 are more or less confined to the stinging nettle and its close relatives.

Mates
The main attractant for those seeking a mate is, of course, the opposite sex. The main ways in which a garden can influence this is simply by making it attractive to the species, so that there is a better chance of finding a mate. This really comes down therefore to the other features – food, homes and shelter.

Homes
These may be more or less permanent or used only for given periods. The first include dead wood, in which many beetle larvae and fungi live, loose bark on trees, logs, stones and water (see Chapter 9).

Temporary homes include nest-boxes for birds and bumble-bees just for the breeding season (although in the case of bumble-bees this is the whole life of the workers and half the life of the queens), and sites for hibernation, for hedgehogs (heaps of leaves or branches), for dormice (boxes in bramble bushes) and sheds or other protected areas (for butterflies, ladybirds and lacewing flies).

Shelter

Shelter serves mainly as a temporary home but there are some
examples that are not in this category. These include lily leaves under
which fish can hide, rough grass for voles to tunnel under and hedges
for birds to roost in, which all serve the purpose of temporary (even if
regularly used) shelter.

Children also appreciate shelter in a garden, especially such
features as tree houses, which give them a feeling of being part of
nature.

11 Gardens for Children

Most children probably regard gardens as primarily exercise grounds and this may be a good argument for a relatively separate area designed to meet this need. Grass is generally the most hard-wearing ground-cover for outdoor exercise but does not necessarily have to be kept short and certainly does not justify the 'manicuring' treatment so often given to lawns. However, exercise is a three-dimensional activity and provision has to be made for aerial adventures as well, involving bodies (climbing trees or rocks) and objects (thrown or kicked).

None of this has much to do with natural history, although the need for trees and rocks may offer opportunities to add biological interest. Otherwise, many children probably consider the garden to be boring – especially their own, familiar garden: in any case, it is what grown-ups talk about! This has partly to do with the more exciting alternatives on offer from modern technology but is also partly because of an understandable ignorance of all that a garden contains. If some of these hidden facets are revealed, many children – as with adults – are both surprised and interested.

So there are three main questions here: first, what would appeal to children in ordinary gardens, if they could see them through the eyes of a naturalist? Secondly, how could gardens be changed to make them more interesting to children? Thirdly, what opportunities are there for children to make their own gardens?

Ordinary gardens

Most gardens are quite small and fully occupied with the plants that the owners find attractive and easy to grow. However, as described in earlier chapters, there are all sorts of interesting creatures associated with these plants if you take the trouble to look and, as I have pointed out, you rarely do this unless you believe that there is actually something to see.

What there is to see will vary with the season. Let us start with midsummer and the most prominent feature – the flowers. The most obvious bits of natural history are the insects on or visiting the flowers and the most easily seen are bees and butterflies.

The best way to engage a child's interest is to pose questions. For example:

What are the butterflies doing?

How are they feeding?

Is that their tongue?

What are they getting with their long tongues?

Why do flowers produce nectar?

Why do they want to attract butterflies?

Why do they need to be pollinated?

Where does the pollen go?

What happens after that?

Why are seeds produced?

How are they distributed?

What are the bees doing?

Are all the bees the same?

Are they all doing the same thing?

Why do they collect pollen?

Where are their young?

Is pollen a good food for them?

The list of questions is endless: the idea is simply to start children asking them.

Let us take a different example – in late winter. It looks as though little is happening and there are few signs of life. Why not ask:

Are all the leaves dead?

On all the trees?

On the lawn?

In the flower beds?

Why are some still green?

Why are some frosted and others not?

Are there any buds on trees and bushes?
What is inside them?
Why don't they burst and grow?
What are they waiting for?
Are there any insects about?
Why not?
Where do they come from in the spring?
Can you find any hiding, in the house, in sheds, in cracks in tree
    bark or under stones?
What do you find under stones?
How many legs do they have?
Are they insects then? (All insects have six legs.)
What do they live on?
Why haven't they disappeared?

You could take any month in the year and devise a list of questions.
Other lists can start with a plant or an animal.

Plant
    What do its leaves do?
    Is anyone eating them?
    Where are they and when do they eat the leaves?
    Are they hiding under the leaf?
    Is the plant a weed?
    How did it get there?

Animal
    What is it?
    Where is it living?
    Why is it there?
    Is it safer?
    What does it eat?
    What eats it?
    Does it have wings? Or legs?
    How many?
    Is it brightly coloured?
    Why?
    Or camouflaged?

The same approach can be taken to a pond, a wall or almost any garden feature and it does not have to be based on what you can see.

Smelling things
Why do some flowers smell and others not?

Does smell attract pollinators?

Is a smell that is attractive to us (for example mint) also attractive to insects, or does it put them off?

Why do leaves smell?

Does it help an insect to identify a food plant?

Can birds smell? All of them? Any of them? Why not?

Beyond the formal features of ordinary gardens there are other opportunities to explore if the garden contains any wilder, less cultivated bits. This is particularly so for the invertebrates and, after all, birds and mammals rarely stay long enough to engage a child's attention.

One solution for birds is to provide well-placed and well-designed nest boxes and bird tables. Children can not only look after the latter but also design and make them. Ideally children's bird tables should be of a height that allows them to put out food but that is out of reach to dogs and cats.

Nest boxes can easily be observed and even the nesting material and food brought for the young can be distinguished. After the young have departed, the nesting material can be examined in detail. (It is worth remembering that there will also be bird parasites, such as fleas!)

Children often have less entrenched biases against creepy-crawlies (although some can be very frightened by quite harmless creatures) and are very receptive to new dimensions. For example, children rapidly grasp the notion that most animals have to hide away in order to survive, and will therefore be found under logs, flat stones, loose bark and leaves, in holes and under water. As soon as this is pointed out, children of all ages, will start looking under everything and spotting holes (in the soil, on paths, in walls, in trees) that are not at all obvious (see Table 11.1).

The human mind, like the human eye, cannot possibly focus on all that it sees, so unless we are actually looking for something we may not see it at all. So a garden is made more interesting to children if

Table 11.1 Animals in hiding

Under stones	Ants
	Slugs
	Centipedes
Under logs	Earthworms
	Slugs
	Centipedes
	Millipedes
	Newts
	Toads
In holes in the ground	Mice, voles and shrews
	Bumble-bees
	Solitary bees and wasps
In holes in trees	Woodpeckers
	Wrens
	Starlings
	Nuthatches
	Great tits
	Blue tits
	Wasps
	Hornets
In very small holes	Beetles
	Wood wasps
	Solitary bees

logs and stones are deliberately placed in order to be looked under. This has to be a deliberate plan in order to avoid the destructive dismemberment of desirable garden features that serve other purposes! This idea can be taken much further, as I discovered, largely by chance, in my own garden – with old dustbin lids.

The diary of the dustbin lids

The idea arose because I left an upturned plastic bucket on a piece of rough grass for some months. On lifting it, I discovered that short-tailed field voles (*Microtus agrestis*, see Figure 11.1) had constructed a nest, largely of moss, with a network of tunnels, some under the grass and some into the soil, leading into and away from the nest. So I left the bucket in place and sometimes on lifting it up I surprised one or, exceptionally, two voles underneath.

Figure 11.1 Field vole
at the entrance to its nest under a dustbin lid

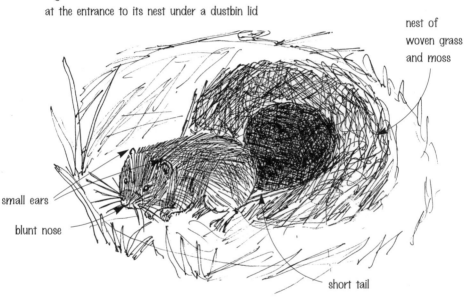

nest of woven grass and moss

small ears

blunt nose

short tail

After a time, it occurred to me to put down other buckets and, especially successfully, old dustbin lids. In due course, nearly all became occupied by voles, nests and tunnels. Recent activity could be gauged by small piles of faecal pellets, changes in the shape of a nest or new holes and tunnels, and the presence of food stores (rose hips, sycamore seeds, cut grass) or their remains.

I then became puzzled by the appearance of empty shells of the banded snail and droppings of a different character (darker, not obviously pelleted and moist). This was resolved when I found common shrews present when I lifted a lid. These animals are easily distinguished, as shown in Figures 11.1, 11.3 and 11.4. Mice have pointed noses, large ears and long tails: voles have blunt noses, small ears and short tails: shrews have very elongated, narrow noses and are a darker brown colour on the upper side. Shrews are primarily insectivorous but also eat snails, and their droppings reflect the animal diet. Voles are mainly vegetarians and this shows in their faecal pellets. I could not tell whether the voles and shrews were sharing or whether, as I suspected, the shrews had taken over.

As half-a-dozen dustbin lids were occupied at any one time, it is obvious that these small animals find them attractive. They clearly recognize the protection afforded, from big animals, birds, rain and so on; they may like the dark and the warmth (black plastic lids trap quite a lot of heat) and the fact that although the soil remains moist the area is dry.

Insects also congregated, especially ants, and woodlice, and spiders. Quite unexpectedly, however, the inhabitants turned out to include bumble-bees, which became obvious when I investigated a vole's nest that turned out to have been occupied by the moss carder-bee (*Bombus muscorum*), so called because they weave a mossy or grassy nest above ground, in which to rear their brood. The nest is made initially by the queen (the only one to overwinter) who sits on, and incubates, the first eggs to be laid – which generate the first workers.

Subsequently, other lids became occupied by carder-bees and, in one case, by short-haired bumble-bees (*Bombus subterraneus*), which built their nests underground, using a vole's tunnels. Around each of the nests occupied by bees, numerous woodlice (of the type that roll up – see Box 11.1) started breeding, perhaps attracted by the dampness, darkness and decaying vegetation (grass rotting in the dark) – so much so that they could be found at any time.

By this time, I was inspecting these lids frequently and, on a cold morning in late spring, discovered a grass snake measuring 45 cm (18 in) long coiled up on top of a mossy nest (see Figure 11.2). When the day warmed up it went out but returned again later until, perhaps unhappy about the inspections, it left, only to move to another dustbin lid less than 2 m (6½ ft) away. Subsequently two grass snakes decided that it was a good place for mating.

Different animals now also use these lids, often for short periods, and on one occasion I surprised a family of four wood mice (*Apodemus sylvaticus*) – also called the long-tailed field mouse (see Figure 11.3); shrews also occur (see Figure 11.4).

Box 11.1 Woodlice

Woodlice are not insects but crustaceans, like crabs and lobsters, with hard external carapaces and legs (for example seven pairs) on the abdomen as well as the thorax. Land forms are not so numerous as those living in water (salt or fresh) but they all breathe through gills.

There are 42 species in the UK but the commonest species in gardens are probably *Oniscus* spp. and *Porcellio* spp., the flattened type with a rough carapace, and *Armadillidium vulgare*, the pill-bug, which is darker grey, shiny and rolls itself into a ball when disturbed. The rolled-up ball looks pretty impregnable but there is actually a woodlouse spider that specializes in attacking this species (see below).

Woodlice all tend to live in dark, damp cracks and crevices under logs and stones, because desiccation is their biggest problem. They generally feed on decaying vegetable and rarely damage growing plants. The eggs, produced during the summer, are carried by the females in a pouch for about two months. The young have fewer legs and are very pale-coloured.

Armadillidium vulgare
(pill bug, length 14–18 mm/ 1/2–3/4 in)

actual size of the
animal when rolled up

The adventure continues but it has already demonstrated (a) that there are ways of seeing creatures you did not know were about, (b) that there are signs of life that can be seen all the time, even when no animals are visible and (c) providing a home limits where you have to look to discover what is going on and to show it to others.

Of course, to see voles, for example, the lid has to be placed on rough grass (not the lawn) and, preferably, over one of the regular

Figure 11.2 Grass snake
coiled under a dustbin lid

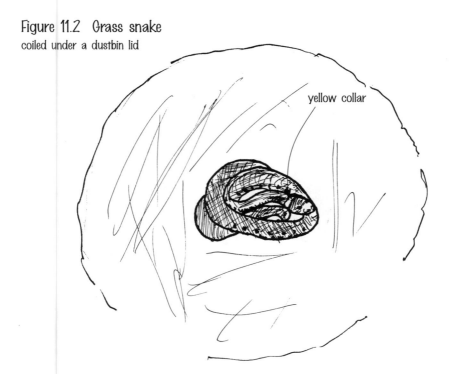

yellow collar

Figure 11.3 Wood mouse
showing its characteristic large ears, pointed nose and long tail

Figure 11.4 Common shrew
at the entrance to its nest: note its very
long, whiskery snout

surface runs or tunnels. For bees and snakes, a wider range of sites
may work, although a covered access area may be needed. In the
years that I have been deploying an increasing number of dustbin
lids, an even greater variety of small creatures have used them. If
food (for example bread or apple) is placed under them, it will
generally disappear within days, even from sites that show no other
signs of occupancy.

It appears that the darkness created is important and covers that let
in any light do not work very well (and become crammed with
somewhat etiolated vegetation). Black ants will use the covers and
build up substantial nests, right up to the 'roof'. Since they obviously
regard the whole thing as being underground, lifting the lid reveals
the inside of the nest, with eggs and pupae as well as adults. If a
cover is placed on short grass, yellow ants may build above ground.
Sometimes the lids collect a great many slugs (and thus may serve as
a slug trap) and spiders will be seen on the tops of the lids,
illustrating the large numbers present in the garden but not usually
visible.

The same or other, novel, techniques could be tried in different
situations, but they all flow from the simple notion of 'looking under
a stone'. The effect on children is considerable: it is almost literally

opening a door on to a different world, a world that is actually there anyway but normally undetected. The most spectacular occasion was when I found a fully grown grass snake early in the morning of a school visit day. It was sufficiently cool that I felt sure it would still be there when the children arrived. And so it was! After due discussion and arranging the children in a ring around the dustbin lid, I lifted it and the snake was revealed (see Figure 11.5). It soon decided to slither out and find a more private hiding place. As planned, the children stayed quite still as it passed between them. One of the teachers did admit to having her eyes closed, but everyone else saw it clearly.

Figure 11.5 Grass snake
departing from its dustbin lid hiding place

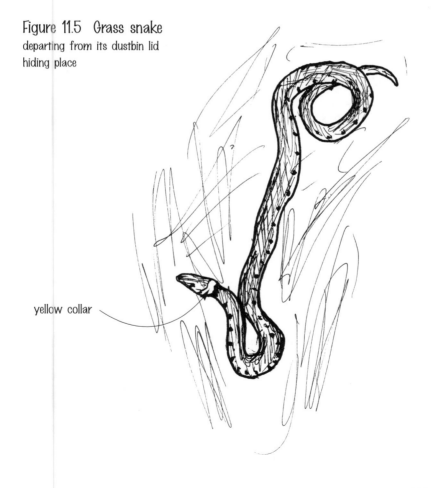

yellow collar

School pond

Ponds and lakes also present opportunities to explore and discover new worlds. Following a visit to the local primary school, St Nicholas Hurst, to show the children what was in their own pond, I came to the conclusion that most such ponds are not designed for this purpose. The main faults are (a) they are too small, especially the perimeter, so that few children can get near the edge, (b) they are too murky, so that nothing can be seen, (c) they are too far from face to water surface and (d) there are no shallow areas for greater visibility.

I therefore constructed, in my own adjacent garden, a pond for children to visit (called 'School Pond'). It has the following key features:

(a) It is long and narrow, so that well over 20 children can line the edges;

(b) It is mainly built above ground, with raised earth banks, so that the children can view it within centimetres of the water surface;

(c) Its banks and edges are covered with smooth branches (poles), forming a curved surface with a flat top, so that children can sit on it or drape themselves over it;

(d) The water has deep areas for water-lilies and for animals to hide in, but also extensive shallows where animals can be easily seen. It is therefore possible to catch aquatic beetles, newts and so on and release them in the shallows, where they can be observed before they disappear into the depths;

(e) The water is kept clear by maintaining high populations of small animals that eat the algae;

(f) There are no fish, as these do limit the populations of small animals;

(g) At each end, there are upright posts supporting a long, small (that is, less than 20 years old) dead elm tree. It is covered with creeper, such as honeysuckle, and its main function is to discourage ducks from flying in: they add nothing, since they do not stay long, but they are destructive of practically all other forms of life. However, the cross piece also illustrates the shallow furrows made by the elm bark beetle larvae that spread the fungus that killed the tree (see Figure 7.1).

(h) A few potted bog plants – yellow iris (*Iris pseudacorus*), rushes, (*Juncus* spp.) and bulrush (*Typha latifolia*) provide botanically interesting but, more importantly, upright leaves for emerging dragonfly and other insects. The dried-out nymphal cases stand out, some 15 – 30 cm (6 – 12 in) above the water, and remain for weeks or even months;

(h) The pond is so constructed that it cannot easily be damaged. The edges are tough and do not contain valuable plants. The most appreciated edge plant is the wild strawberry, with little height, spread by long runners and bearing edible fruit over a long season.

Virtually all the pond inhabitants mentioned in Chapter 9 are to be found in School Pond but their numbers vary enormously. The ways in which the children (aged 5–11) see the pond and its inhabitants are illustrated in Figures 11.6, 11.7 and 11.8

Snails breed for most of the year, so all sizes are to be seen most of the time. *Daphnia* and *Cyclops* vary greatly in their numbers and surface feeders such as whirligig beetles appear for a few days and then fly off again. Pond-skaters seem to breed continuously over a long season but water-boatmen fluctuate between large numbers of adults and large numbers of young ones. Frogs and newts are, of course, seasonal visitors but their tadpoles (and 'newtpoles') are present for several months. All these changes mean that there is always a mixture of recognizable old friends (for example snails) and new faces with interesting life-histories. Just like flat stones, lily leaves can be turned over to see not only the snail eggs but the developing young within their transparent jelly. This is true for frog- and toad-spawn in a pond where no part of the surface is very far from a bank. The pond thus functions as an established focal point for wildlife, much of which can be discovered just by leaning over the banks.

It is helpful if the pond is not dauntingly large. Most of us adjust our viewing to the scale of the scene. When we look at mountains, we see no detail, and when we look at a large lake, we are less inclined to look at the detail in the shallows at the edge. So, especially for small children, scale is important, and an appropriate scale is easier to relate to and feel confident about.

School wood

The right scale is particularly important for trees. Experience of

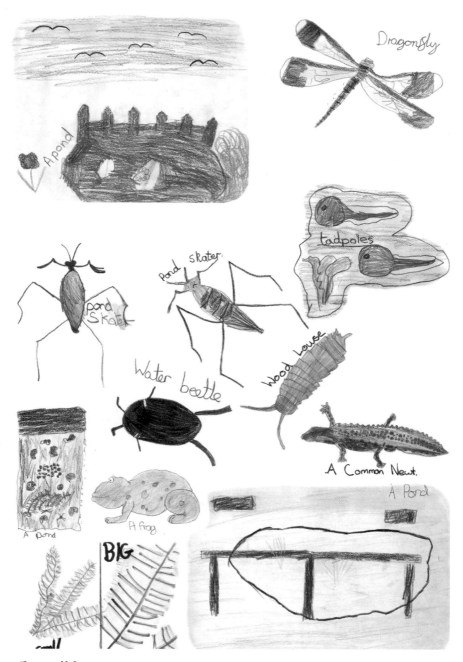

Figure 11.6   The pond and some of its inhabitants

Figure 11.7
This drawing has a flap at the top, which is shown lifted to reveal the inhabitants (some apparently asleep!)

Figure 11.8
This drawing shows the circular depressions in the water surface caused by the pond-skaters' feet

School Pond led me to think about a School Wood, in which all the trees were stopped at heights of 1 – 1.5 m (3¼ – 5 ft), so that all parts could be examined closely – bark, buds, leaves, caterpillars, fruits and seeds. These take some time to establish but even a couple of years is enough to produce stocky, tough little trees, since all the growth is forced into a small-sized plant.

However, the children do not need to be presented with a finished product before their interest begins. There is great fun to be had from doing the planting. This does not have to wait until some optimum time – after all, tree seeds simply fall on the ground, though some (mainly acorns) are buried by squirrels and jays. All that is needed is some space and, since most seeds just land on the surface, planting

---

Table 11.2 Tree seeds

The following are all easy for children to identify and grow (all come up quite naturally near or in woods).

Tree	Seed
Horse chestnut *Aesculus hippocastanum*	In spring green fruit with spikes, ripening in the autumn when they contain the well-known chestnut-coloured conkers
Oak *Quercus* spp.	Acorn in cup
Sycamore *Acer pseudoplatanus*	'Helicopter' seeds in bunches
Lime *Tilia* spp.	Wing with stalked, spherical seed
Ash *Fraxinus excelsior*	Winged seeds in bunches
Hawthorn *Crataegus monogyna*	In fruit (haw)
Yew *Taxus baccata*	In sticky red berry
Cherry *Prunus* spp.	Stone in fruit
Holly *Ilex aquifolium*	Seed in berry
Rowan *Sorbus aucuparia* (mountain ash)	Seed in red berries
Beech *Fagus sylvatica*	1–3 nuts in husk

Figure 11.9 Tree fruits carrying seeds

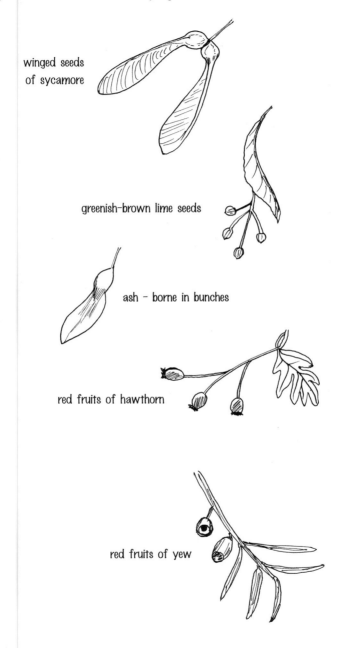

winged seeds
of sycamore

greenish-brown lime seeds

ash – borne in bunches

red fruits of hawthorn

red fruits of yew

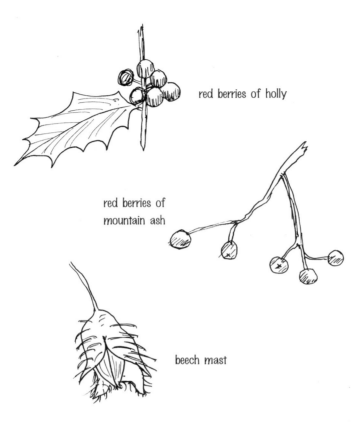

red berries of holly

red berries of
mountain ash

beech mast

depth is not critical. Tree seedlings have their own ways of adjusting depth of seed. It is a good idea to encourage planting in quite excessive numbers, so that samples can be dug up regularly to see what is happening, to observe the astonishingly strong root growth that may pull the seed down and, in the case of tap roots (like oak), get so deep that they can survive very dry weather.

Conkers and acorns are familiar to all, but ash, lime and sycamore are easily recognized and collected (see Table 11.2). Stopping the leading shoot can be done whenever one wishes to see what will happen – usually it overcomes the dormancy of lower buds, which branch out to produce very bushy little trees. These develop quite thick stems and, once they are well established, are not easily damaged.

However, it is not only living trees that are of interest in a wood.

Dead wood – branches dying back, old tree stumps or fallen logs – is actually full of life. A great many creatures, especially the larvae of beetles, spend years burrowing in dead wood, feeding on it. These include stag beetle larvae (some of our largest larvae and most spectacular beetles) and the larvae of wasp-beetles (*Clytus ariestis*), which, although harmless, gain protection from their black and yellow coloration. Very old stumps practically fall apart, revealing a network of tunnels. Fungi also grow on dead wood and produce very attractive reproductive bodies. Children are generally surprised at how very hard some of them can become, especially the shelf-like bracket fungi.

Woodland leaf litter is full of interesting creatures, serves as a protective mulch for seedlings (for example from conkers), and in winter, attracts birds such as blackbirds and flocks of redwings (winter visitors) to search for food. Very often the first sign is dead leaves being flung about and, in very hard frosts, these leaves may be the only movable objects.

A children's garden

The idea of planting and watching plants grow does not have to be limited to trees, of course. A children's garden (as opposed to a garden for children) does not have to be specified, since the object is to allow freedom to grow whatever the young gardener wants or is interested in. Some children will want to copy an orthodox garden (flower or vegetable) but others will want to do something different. There appear to be two basic principles, however.

First, most children want to be individually creative, to feel that, whatever they do, it is their own and they are the only judge of their work. Admiration may be called for but the essential is to show interest – rather than curiosity. Secondly, childhood moves very quickly and a year is an enormous proportion of a child's life, so whatever they want to do, try or see, may be quite different in a few months' time.

The scale of whatever is done has to be appropriate to age (and other attributes, probably): the child has to be able to relate to his or her own garden. Furthermore, it may be best to start very small, say with a garden tub (or even a big plant pot), in order to get the hang of it and discover what can be done.

If this is a first attempt at creating a garden, rapid results are essential. That is why cress seeds on damp paper indoors are so successful: children can always see whether anything is happening and get used to the idea of seeds developing, so that seeds out of sight in soil are not so discouraging. Even so, it is best to start with those that germinate quickly and, above all, soon produce brightly coloured flowers. Especially good at this are annuals, such as nasturtium.

Plants with scented leaves

Leaves are plentiful for much of the year, so some can be removed and crushed at any time. Mints are a good example and include common mint, bog mint (requires damp soil) and catmint. Trees such as balsam poplar should be easily grown from cuttings or suckers and can be kept small.

Plants that attract butterflies

Red, purple and blue flowers with nectar (especially *Buddleja* species and varieties) attract butterflies to feed but relatively few orthodox garden plants are suitable for their larvae (except cabbages!). To attract butterflies to lay their eggs, plant ivy (flowering), nettles, docks, wild grasses, thistles, and cuckoo flowers.

Very attractive plants are:

Plant	Special feature
Scarlet pimpernel	square stems
Wild strawberry	edible fruit
Foxglove	attracts bumble-bees
Cranesbill	interesting seeds
Herb robert	interesting seeds
Meadowsweet	original source of aspirin (with willow)
Meadow vetchling	climbs in long grass
Burdock	hooked seeds

Great willow herb	tall (plant at the back)
Dog violet	no scent
Green alkanet	smothers even nettles
Borage	useful herb
Self-heal	leaves used for healing wounds in the Middle Ages
Feverfew	recommended as migraine relief
Goatsbeard	flowers only open on sunny mornings (called 'Jack-go-to-bed-at-noon')
Catsear	furry leaves

All grow readily on suitable soil and require no attention.

Plants that attract birds

In this country, it is mainly seed heads that attract birds, especially goldfinches on thistles and bullfinches hovering to collect dandelion seeds, but there are always birds that will visit any part of any garden to hunt for food such as insects, spiders, snails, earthworms and so on.

Plants with different-shaped stems

Cross section	Plant
Square	Labiates: mint, dead-nettle, self-heal
Triangular	Sedges
Circular	Willowherb, meadowsweet
Circular but filled with pith	Rushes (used for rush lights in Middle Ages)

Aquatic plants

Even in a very small pond, only 1 m (3¹/₄ ft) across, water-starwort and Canadian pondweed will attract newts; frogs will spawn and a host of insects will breed. Made in a plastic lined hollow, a pond can be surrounded by a boggy area, thus creating a bog garden.

A bog garden

A bog garden has to be kept moist and will grow rushes, bog mint, yellow iris (flags), kingcups (marsh marigold), water forget-me-not, marsh yellowcress, purple loosestrife and gipsywort, as well as liverworts and all kinds of moss.

Conservation and educational

Gardens also present opportunities for conservation and older children might enjoy the opportunity to help in a worthwhile project to record the presence of creatures whose numbers are declining (for example stag beetles and dormice) or to help in preserving some of the rarer species. However, such possibilities do not fit easily into very small gardens.

Teachers of biology or science could make more use of gardens, in two main ways. First, they are, as I have tried to show, a good place to encourage the art of discovery (but see Box 11.2) – and it is something of an art, since neither what to look for nor how to see it are obvious without some help and guidance. However, just a very few pointers can release the inquisitive questioning accompanied by acute observation which are at the heart of the natural sciences.

Box 11.2 Risks

Exploring gardens in the UK carries relatively little risk. Virtually everyone is aware of nettles, wasps and bees and children are usually warned about handling them. Wasps rarely attack unless provoked and bees even less so: but hornets are a different matter. They are larger than wasps and the black coloration of the wasp is replaced by brown. They have a powerful sting and, in my painful experience, will attack without warning and without provocation. Furthermore, they fly straight at you. I have had three hornets' nests in crevices or weather-boarding of my house, one of them within 30 cm (12 in) of my front door. I had to wear protective clothing to get rid of them, which took several days each time, because there were also some inside that I could not reach. At the first hint of my approach, they swarmed out and successive individuals bashed into my hard hat!

Nettles, fortunately behave rather better. The main problems with plants is with the poisonous parts. It is best not to eat any of the wild berries, except those of wild strawberry, elderberry and blackberry. Leaves may also be poisonous (see Box 8.4) and some can cause a rash if they are touched (some types of *Salvia*).

Secondly, guided garden visits can be used to stimulate a different way of looking at the world, leading to a desire to learn more about what is seen. There are, of course, limits to what can be seen: large parts of the natural history of a garden remain hidden or are not on view during any particular visit. Books and classroom teaching can then be related to what has been seen and open yet more windows on a world that could have been seen or, perhaps, will never be seen. What could be more educational than inspiring a spirit of discovery and a wish to learn more?

The 'ideal' children's garden

Figures 11.6, 11.7, 11.8 were drawn by younger children (aged five to seven years). The older children (aged eight years) were asked to draw their ideal garden, though the title they actually used varied a bit. Two things stood out in all these brightly coloured drawings (see Figures 11.10, 11.11 and 11.12). First, they combined play features (such as tree-houses, swings, climbing frames) with wildlife features and, among the latter, every one included a pond. And over the years, I have noticed that, whatever else they see, such as nests (of birds, wasps, bumble-bees, voles), interesting plants and seeds, eggs (of birds, newts, snails), fox-holes or flowers, School Pond is always the centre of interest.

Figure 11.10 Max's 'ideal garden'

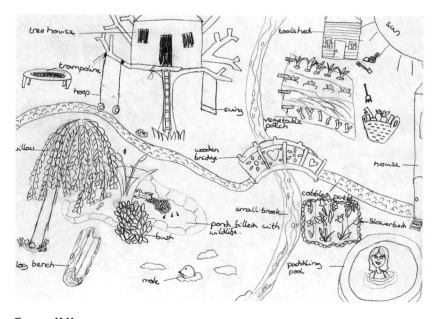

Figure 11.11 The pond (with frog spawn) in a large garden

Figure 11.12   The 'dazzerling' garden

Conversion Factors

Linear

$1\mu m = 0.001$ m $= 0.01$ mm

1 mm = 0.04 in   1 in = 25. 40 mm

1m = 3.28 ft   1 ft = 0.30 m

1 km = 0.62 mile   1 mile = 1.61 km

1 km = 1000 m

Area

1 ha = 2.47 acres   1 acre = 0.40 ha

1 ha = 10,000 m^2

1 m^2 = 10.764 sq ft

1 km^2 = 0.39 miles

Mass

1 kg = 2.20 lb   1 lb = 0.45 kg

Volume

1 litre (water) = 2.20 lb   1 lb (water) = 0.45 litre

1 litre (water) = 0.26 US gal   1 US gal = 3.79 litre

1 litre (water) = 0.22 Imperial gal
   (8.33 lb)

$10^2 = 100$

$10^3 = 1,000$

$10^4 = 10,000$

$10^6 = 1$ million

$10^9 = 1$ billion

Abbreviations

C	carbon
Ca	calcium
Cl	chlorine
CO_2	carbon dioxide
Cu	copper
DM	dry matter
Fe	Iron
ft	feet
g	gram
H	hydrogen
ha	hectare
in	inch
kg	kilogram
km	kilometre
m.	million
m	metre
mm	millimetre
μm	micrometre
N	nitrogen
Na	sodium
O	oxygen
P	phosphorus
ppm	parts per million
Si	silicon

Glossary

aestivation	Dormancy during summer or dry season.
association	Grouping of individuals with some interaction but well short of specialized relationships such as parasitism or symbiosis.
carnivores	Animals that feed on other animals or on material of animal origin.
chloroplasts	Discrete photosynthetic organelles within plant cells, containing chlorophyll.
colony	A social group living together, with varying degrees of co-operation between individuals.
community	A social group within a circumscribed area.
conservation	Protection and preservation of species or their habitats.
coprophagy	Consumption of own faeces (refection in the rabbit).
crepuscular	Appearing or active in twilight.
detrivores	Animals that feed on dead plant or animal material.
development	Sequential organizational changes in an organism of a qualitative kind, often associated with growth.
ecology	The study of organisms in relation to their environment.
ecosystems	Systems which include both living and non-living substances interacting to produce an exchange of materials between them.
ecto-parasite	A parasite which lives on the outside of its host.
endo-parasite	A parasite which lives within the body of its host.

evapo-transpiration	Loss of water by evaporation and transpiration from the above-ground parts of the plant.
exoskeleton	External skeleton (as in insects and crabs)– a hard outer covering.
genetic modification (manipulation or engineering)	The science of modifying the genetic constitution of plants and animals directly.
halteres	Stalked knobs that replace the hind wings in some flying insects.
herbivores	Animals that feed on plant material.
hermaphrodite	Bisexual.
hibernation	Dormancy during winter: metabolism is greatly slowed, and in mammals temperature drops close to that of their surroundings.
homeotherms	Warm-blooded animals whose temperature is maintained above that of their usual surroundings.
hormone	A secretion within an organism that affects various body functions.
humus	Complex organic component of the soil, resulting from decomposition of plant and animal tissues.
hyphae	Fungal filaments.
inquiline	Animal living in the home of another (a commensal).
invertebrates	Animals without backbones.
meristem	A group of actively-growing cells, for example at the apex of a grass stem.
mycorrhiza	Fungus associated with the roots of higher plants.
nectivores	Animals that feed on nectar.
nitrogen fixation	The fixation of gaseous nitrogen by bacteria in the roots of, for example, legumes.
nymph	Young of an insect whose bodily structure, at all stages, looks like a miniature adult.

GLOSSARY

omnivores	Animals that feed on material of both plant and animal origin.
ovipositor	A tube at the end of an insect's body, used to deposit an egg. Modified in bees and wasps to form a sting.
organic gardening	Commonly thought of as without the use of manufactured chemicals, but now conforming to very detailed production standards.
parasitoid	An organism in which a free-living female lays its eggs in or on a host resulting in the death of the host.
parthenocarpy	Seed ripening without fertilization.
parthenogenesis	Giving birth to young by self-fertilization.
passerine	Small, perching birds of the order *Passeriformes*, sparrow-like.
pheromone	Chemical substance produced by one individual that affects the behaviour or physiology of another.
pH	Chemical measure of acidity ($<pH7$) and alkalinity ($>pH7$).
photosynthesis	The process by which carbohydrates are manufactured by the chloroplasts of plants from CO_2 and water, using the energy of sunlight.
poikilotherms	Cold-blooded animals, whose body temperature varies, to a large extent depending on their environment.
radicle	Plant root.
refection	Production of soft pellets of excreta that are eaten and thus digested for a second time (see coprophagy).
respiration	The oxidative breakdown and release of energy from fuel molecules by reaction with oxygen in aerobic cells.
runners	Extension of the stem which by rooting at intervals gives rise to new plants.

saprophyte	An organism that lives on dead and decaying organic matter.
senescence	Process in which plant leaves age and die, usually involving chlorophyll degradation.
stamen	The organ of a flower which produces pollen.
stigma	Terminal expansion of the style of a flower which receives pollen.
stolons	Creeping plant stems, above the soil surface.
stomata	Minute, controllable pores in the leaf through which gases and water vapour are exchanged with the atmosphere.
style	The prolongation of the carpel supporting the stigma.
symbiosis	A mutually beneficial relationship (usually close) between two different organisms.
tillers	The branches of grasses.
transpiration	The evaporation of water from plants, mainly through stomata in the leaves.
viviparous	Giving birth to live young.

Additional Reading

There are a huge number of reference books for identifying plants and animals that may be found in gardens but there are very few that are in any way similar to the present book. The nearest is *The Natural History of the Garden* by Michael Chinery, published in 1997 by Fontana/Collins. It is a very comprehensive description of the animals and plants likely to be found in a British garden and contains keys to identify them. Among the other identification keys are the Collins Field Guides (to Britain and Europe) and the naturalists' handbooks published by Richmond Publishing Company Ltd, with titles such as *Insects on Nettles* and *Animals under Logs and Stones*; the Audubon Society's Field Guides to North American Mammals, Birds, Trees and Wildflowers; and the Peterson Field Guides on Mammals, Humming Birds, Reptiles, Insects and so forth, published by Houghton Mifflin, New York.

Books focusing on gardens include:

Grissell, Eric. *Insects and Gardens*. Portland, Oregon: Timber Press, 2002.

Lutz, Frank E. *A Lot of Insects: Entomology in a Suburban Garden*. New York: G. P. Putnam's Sons, 1941.

Owen, Jennifer. *The Ecology of a Garden: the First Fifteen Years* Cambridge, England: Cambridge University Press, 1991.

Books dealing with wider, background topics include:

George, Wilma. *Animal Geography*. London, England: Heinemann, 1952.

Pennycuick, C. J. *Newton Rules Biology*. Oxford, England: Oxford University Press, 1992.

Van Andel, T. H. *New Views on an Old Planet* (2nd ed.). Cambridge, England: Cambridge University Press, 1994.

Index

Page numbers in *italics* refer to pages on which figures appear.

3 4/04